# The Ravens' Song

## A Journey of the Spirit

## Jim Gael

Rockin' K Publishers, LLC

# Special Thanks

I have many people to thank for this book.

Ironically, the first on the list isn't a person. God gave me a gift for language and writing. Thank you, Father.

Next, my amazing family. They've always been supportive of my writing. Thank you Mom, Dad, brother, sister, aunt, uncles, and all of the rest of you. You know who you are.

I couldn't do this without the support of my outstanding friends. They don't want their names mentioned – fair enough – but you know who you are. Thank you for being there for me.

These words are dedicated First and Foremost to...

The Ancestors from whence they came;

The Ancient and Proud People who inspired them;

Those whom they will Inspire;

And those who inspire me still.

For Leading me to the Truth;

For Showing me the Path;

And for Guiding me through the Darkness.

Thank you, All.

# Contents

# Foreword

Much can be – and has been – said of the cultural and spiritual ideals of the ancient Nordic peoples. Many things about these people and their spiritual paths have been twisted – some by competing religions and cultures, some for the sake of backing an unpopular or personal cause, and some just because the proverbial "other guy" won the fight: history is written by the winners, after all. Much has been lost to the sands of time, over the course of countless generations that separate us from our ancient ancestors. Even more has been fabricated to fill in that vast, incomprehensible gap between our modern world and the world of our forebears. Hence, the mythos of the brutal, wandering savage was born.

I was fortunate to know my grandfather until I was an adult. This was a man who fought in and lived through the Second World War, who came home to a wife and children and worked a day job, and somehow found the time and energy and sheer will to come home from that job and the bustle of daily life and build a functioning ranch. You read that correctly: he built our family's farm. This man came home exhausted every single day, like many of us do, and still had the gumption to hand-cut brush and trees to clear pastures; to trim those trees into posts; to dig postholes, set the posts, and stretch barbed wire; to feed cattle and horses and chickens; to check gopher traps; to hop on an old tractor and till the pastures until long after the sun had set; to hunt for food to put on the table; and still spend some time with his family. He was a good man, a strong and stalwart man. He shunned convenience in favor of personal strength and independence. He was one major reason I joined the Army: I had a deep need to emulate him, to be more like him, and to thereby know a little of his strength in myself.

I sometimes still miss him sorely, even though I know that proud, stubborn man is still tending his cattle and feeding them range cubes with a self-satisfied smile while calling them by names like "Sweet Pea." That was Grandpa, and always will be, for me at least.

Don't get me wrong – it wasn't all fun-filled days on the farm and warm smiles and cow-petting. My Grandpa could be a hard man. He believed in hard work, strict discipline, good manners, and no fear. He believed in doing the right thing no matter what it cost you, in honesty and penance. He knew that life was hard, and that you had to be tough – and wise – to do well.

So, why talk about my grandfather? Well, he's one of my ancestors.

The Nordic spiritual path is all about ancestry. It's about knowing where (and who) you come from, and carrying those traditions forward into the future. It's about living your life the way Grandpa lived, even if only some aspects of it, so that you can share in the wisdom and strength your forebears knew. More than anything, it's about drawing on the inspiration past generations have given you to take charge of your own life and make it into something you can be proud of, and remembered for.

As you read this book, I urge you to reflect on your ancestry – and not just the far-flung past, but also your recent ancestors – your parents, grandparents, great-grandparents, uncles, and such. Who are your role models? Who served as your moral compass? Which of them taught you the ideals of home and family? Who do you most want to be like? Which has the most colorful stories? Overcame the hardest circumstances? Who shows the most compassion? Who has the most loyal friends? Which one makes inappropriate jokes?

When you think of your most recent ancestors, you can usually relate one or more of them directly to someone in the Norse pantheon. Loyal and hardy Uncle Thor, who always has your back. Odin, everybody's dad, who's somewhat aloof and terrifying, but only because he's busy providing for your future and keeping you out of trouble. Freyja, your mom, who can be a loving wife, a stern parent, and champion for her children with all the might of a Valkyrie, and who somehow manages to sneak in a little magic here and there that makes it all okay…certainly it is magical how she always seems to know what's going on, though nobody told her. Uncle Loki, who's always making inappropriate jokes until somebody gets their feelings hurt, and who keeps laughing anyway. Uncle Baldur, who is always kind and generous, and whom you know you can always go to for good advice. You get the idea.

My grandfather could never figure out how to work the new television my parents bought him – technology baffled him, and maybe even offended him a little bit. Still, I never once thought of my grandfather as just a dumbfounded, dull, mud-covered savage who wandered around the same tiny patch of land his whole life without bathing or brushing his teeth. So why would I think any different of my ancestors from the distant past? Trust me: having harvested wheat by hand before (I was doing penance for having a smart mouth), I can tell you for a certainty that you don't walk away from that job, with the itchy chaff stuck to every piece of exposed skin, and not jump into the first container of cool water big enough to fit you for a nice bath. I have always been confused by this misconception that our ancestors were somehow less intelligent than ourselves. The knowledge they cultivated was different than ours, more salt of the Earth, more focused on survival, but no less valuable or worthwhile. For example, my grandfather could feed his family without ever going to a grocery store, should the need arise – and he frequently did. How many people do you know today who could do that?

My point? The Old Norse viewed their ancestors as personal heroes, role models for their own lives who were worthy of praise and remembrance. Following the spiritual path of the Old Norse means honoring your ancestors for their triumphs, learning lessons from their mistakes, and following their good examples.

This book is all about challenging your misconceptions about the Nordic spiritual path, and possibly giving you a new perspective on the people who followed it, their ways of life, and their beliefs. It is my personal story. That said, interpret the following tale as you will...and may it serve you as well in the reading as it has served me in living it, and relating it here to you.

~ Jim Gael

# Prologue

## A Dream of War

Imagine being born into absolute chaos and mayhem. Imagine sensory deprivation in reverse. That's how my dream started.

The ground shook, and a roar like a thousand screaming jet engines rent the air around me. I added my own battle roar – primal, and so thunderously loud it hurt my throat and my ears. I threw back my head with the scream, releasing some small measure of the turmoil inside me, and opened my eyes.

The sky was the color of blood, streaked with brilliant shades of fire. Though it was clearly nighttime, I could see no stars. A haze of smoke filled the air, making it difficult to breathe properly, choking me.

Fires burned on the horizon in all directions, their lights too bright, too harsh, blinding me. I stood in a valley, a deep rift in the earth. As I looked around me and took in my surroundings – what I could see of them – I quickly realized that I was surrounded.

Thousands of figures, millions perhaps, crowded in on all sides of me, a vast sea of people-shapes and the shadows they cast in harsh firelight. None of them had any clear definition or features that I could discern. Some moaned, some screamed or wailed, some murmured and muttered, and some whispered. Taken together, they were the source of the roar in the air.

Apparently, my battle yell had gotten the attention of those closest to me. They weren't attacking me so much as pushing in toward me, invading my personal space, the very mass of their collective presence a crushing weight. I fought down feelings of panic and claustrophobia, but it was a close call, and very hard to maintain. None of the figures had any faces, but my instincts told me a great number of them were looking at me: beseeching, accusing, and assessing me with eyes they didn't possess.

For what seemed like an eternity, I stood frozen in fear. The sea of figures around me was endless. I tried closing my eyes, plugging my ears, willing myself to come back to reality – nothing worked. When I opened my eyes, even more figures were paying attention to me. When I unplugged my ears, the roar in the air grew louder. I felt like it would all end, and I could finally have peace, if only I could see the stars, but the chaos around me obscured everything.

It would come to a fight, then. If I wanted to get out of this valley and see the stars, I would have to fight my way through the massed figures that surrounded me and climb my way out. A fight I could handle. Terror faded, just a little, and I felt my resolve harden. I would see the stars.

Two very startling things happened just then.

First, a shield appeared in my hand. It was small and made of heavy wood, like a buckler. It wouldn't help much when the fighting started, but it was more than I had a moment before. Second, the figures backed away from me just a tiny bit, and the world around me became slightly...clearer. The figures nearest me, in front of me, took on a little bit more definition. The sky grew a single shade darker, and I could see the faintest outline of the moon above the ridge at the end of the valley before me. The harsh actinic glare of the fires that blinded me faded the barest lumen. The clamor of the moans, wails, screams, mutters, and whispers dulled by a fraction of a decibel.

I looked up. The moon above the ridge seemed a thousand miles away through an endless uphill sea of strange figures and who knew what other dangers lurking in the blinding half-dark.

I took a step, and then another, and another. The world became clearer by the tiniest degree each time I moved forward. Sometimes the figures would simply move out of my way, fading into the sea of non-faces. Sometimes they would try to push or pull me back, but I continued to push my way through them using the small shield and my own sheer will. The push through the figures became more intense as I went, and I felt sure I would need to fight very soon. The panic began to rise again. How could I possibly fight my way through millions? I pushed the panic away by force of will and took another step.

This was going to be a very long journey. But if I could survive it, if I could make it to the top of that ridge, I could see the stars. I knew it.

I steeled myself and took another step. Whatever it took, I would see the stars.

# Chapter One

My name is....

Well, it doesn't matter. Not much about me personally matters, in any respect. I'm one of billions of people that walk the earth. One of trillions and zillions of creatures that creep, crawl, walk, run, swim, or fly around our little blue speck in the universe. Of course, I have a name, and a family, and a job, and I pay taxes like everyone else. I'm a conscious, self-aware being just like everyone else. And that's the real crux of the matter: when it really boils down to truth, there's absolutely nothing special about me. Even though I feel, somewhere deep down, that I am special. Something that makes me a unique person, a unique soul. Maybe I simply have a human need inside me to be unique and special.

And yet, I am just one of billions that are not special. I like to call them – us – "The Wandering."

I wake up. I eat breakfast. I go to work. I sit in a cube, or frame houses, or sling pizza. I come home. I go to church – whatever that may be for me at the time – on some day of the week. I read, or watch television, or play video games. Sometimes I eat foods that are bad for me or go to the bar and get drunk. A lot of the time, I try to eat healthy (or at least restrain my urges for more nachos and beer), try to not drink too much, try to pray, try to...well, and try to do "the right thing."

Just like everyone else.

I try, and I try. And still I wander.

Why do I wander? Why does anyone wander? I have a theory about that.

We're all looking for that something that makes us special and unique, that means we have a value more than monetary. We're looking for a roadmap to salvation and spiritual security, or immortality – something that means we don't have to stop existing when we die, that we can go to some version of paradise and live on, in one form or another, forever. We're looking for more than that, though – we're looking for an intuitive and natural way to *live*, in this life. Something that feels right. We're looking for "the right thing."

But what is "the right thing?" Any of the various flavors of Christianity? Buddhism? Taoism? Islam? None of them? A combination of all of them? Which religion is "right?" There are so many different options, and if you choose the wrong one, you're screwed. That's the question The Wandering constantly ask ourselves. It's also the wrong question.

I was raised in a Christian home. Everybody I ever knew growing up was one flavor of Christian or another: Catholics, Methodists, Baptists, Lutherans, and the rare Episcopalian. I myself was baptized Lutheran, but was raised and confirmed in the Methodist church. As I grew into adolescence, I started to notice the similarities between a church and a social club or clique. Even within our church, there were little cliques: the old veterans hung together, the farmers hung together, the socialites hung together...and the junior high kids hung out with the same people they hung out with in school. Which was to say, not me. Never was this church/clique similarity more pronounced for me than one year when I was in middle school, and I attended a week of Bible School during the summer.

In school, I was something of a reject – I got picked on, sure, but it was more than that. It was more like negligence. These people wouldn't give me the time of day, except to ridicule me in one way or another. In turn, I tried to lay low and avoid them. That means I had never even talked to some of the people in my Sunday school class before, even though they were in my grade and we went to a very small school in a small town. They honestly didn't know anything about me, and had never spoken to me before. Perhaps I should specify that the people in this Sunday school class, that went to my church, were not my tormentors in school; I just didn't know them, and some of them hung out with a few of the people that did torment me. These people had never participated in my humiliation before, however.

For those not familiar with the experience of going to a Methodist church (or any Christian institution), there's a very clear separation between when you're in church and when you're not. In church, everybody's the same – we're all sinners, and we're all in this together. So, everybody in the church should be equal to everybody else. At least, in theory. This being the case, I took this chance at Sunday school to pull my head out of the sand and introduce myself to some of my peers for the first time. I chose a somewhat inopportune moment to express my intelligence and curious nature during a conversation, and there it was: they laughed, they humiliated me, and we were back to junior high cliques and the cruelty of teenagers again. So where was the separation of church and school? Where was I supposed to fit in *now*? My one safe haven, where everyone was supposed to be unique and beautiful and treasured was lost to me. I put up with their weekly torture for a few more years, and hated them sorely for it, until I had a choice and decided I wasn't going anymore. By that time, I didn't just hate them, I hated all people my age, and the church to boot. How could people be so cruel and hurtful? How could the people who ran the church allow that kind of thing to go on – not for an afternoon, but for *years*?

Needless to say, I left the church. I felt sorry for myself, and after a few months of screaming at God for being so mean to me, and for letting others be so mean to me, I stopped really believing. It didn't fit me, not really. It seemed like a sham, a lie. When I thought back to my past, to all the times I had prayed or demanded or anything else – any attempt to feel or see God's presence in my life whatsoever – I couldn't find anything that would convince me anyone was listening.

So, I wandered.

I've always been interested in culture, since I was a young child. I wrote an awesome paper about Texas history when I was still in early elementary school. I love the story of the Alamo and Gonzales. I love stories about the Old West. Probably I got so interested in history and how cultures shape it and the people of ancient times because I wanted to make some sense out of my own past. Where did I come from? I remember some things about my biological father, but he wasn't around much after my mom booted him out when I was two or three, and when I was five my mom married my stepfather. I always felt like a little bit of an outsider in my own family because of that – I had a different dad that apparently wanted nothing to do with me. Why was that? What made me...well, *me*? My stepfather's family was German (that would be Grandpa, from the prologue), but that never quite sat right with me. After all, I had *red* hair, and sharper cheekbones than everyone else. I looked different, thought differently. I could see the appeal, in a way, but I was certain my ancestors weren't entirely German.

I started questing after my ancestry right around the time I was exorcised from the company of my peers and gave up trying to fit in with any one group for good. Sure, there were a few guys I hung out with in high school – we even had a band – but I never really felt like I was part of the group. I wondered if maybe I had some kind of family history of this type of social condition. So, I started looking for my ancestors. I didn't find them for the longest time. I was in college by the time I asked the right person the right question, and it had been right under my nose the whole time. My mother's mother told me that our side of the family was Scots-Irish and Welsh (possibly Manx). That made much more sense to me, and I started digging. I found out that on my biological father's side, I'm one-eighth Comanche.

Scots-Irish, Comanche, and a tiny bit of German and Manx. No *wonder* I had anger issues and trouble fitting in.

Oh, come on. That was funny.

That's when I really got the bug. I had to know more about these people in my past, my ancestors: where they came from, how they lived, what they ate...and what they believed.

Everything I found simply confused me. I mean, come on: at least the Christian beliefs are pretty uniform and tell a single story that has a point. Theologically speaking, it's fairly easy to understand. The Native American, Norse, and Celtic beliefs? I couldn't even clearly *identify* any beliefs. They were just collections of random stories that, while some of them obviously had a moral, were seemingly disjointed and unrelated. It was hard to find anything detailed or comprehensible at all about the Native American beliefs, and they seemed to vary widely by tribe. The Norse stories, on first inspection, sounded like somebody writing the strangest thesis paper ever while three sheets to the wind and high as a kite at a particularly secular frat party. The Celtic stories read like the weirdest season of a soap opera ever penned by a desperate author on what must have been a wonderful LSD trip. Also, I'm pretty sure there was plenty of alcohol involved.

Seriously? *Seriously, people?* I come looking for the answers to the mysteries of life and death and afterlife and *this* is what you hand me? Surely this was a joke.

So – again – I wandered.

If people asked, I just said "Christian" or "scientist," depending on how logically-oriented I felt that day. I even kept up the charade of believing – and maybe, in spurts, I truly did – but it never really took root. I could believe the stories, I could believe the Bible even, without any reservation. I just couldn't feel any connection between myself and the Divine.

The only place I found any peace at all in those days was out in the wilds of the Earth...which means, of course, the places I was familiar with from my child-hood and near the college I attended *and* that I could afford enough gas money to reach. I would drive out to somewhere there were not a lot of people around – no people, if I could find such a place – and I would sit, and write, and read, and sing, and build little forts to hang out in with little stone thrones for me to sit upon.

Don't judge me. I was a troubled youth. Obviously.

Joking aside, this was a clue. Another piece of the great puzzle fell into place for me that, looking back, had always been right there in front of me. Something true about myself, something important to me, that I hadn't taken note of before. I found peace only when I was out in nature somewhere.

This was the only thing that ever felt right to me.

I took solace in the woods, and I read, and played, and watched Nature in all its glory. And I prayed.

So why was I still one of The Wandering?

I had to dig deeper, try harder, to break the cycle and find some direction.

# Chapter Two

The problem with religion is that it's full of rules.

Note that I didn't mention spirituality or faith. Religion is something entirely separate: it's a system of order imposed upon spirituality. It's a set of rules. Don't steal. Be a "good" person and love your neighbor, just don't screw your neighbor's wife. Try not to kill anybody. And of course, every religion's most favorite rule of all: *this* is the only "right" religion. Translated as: "if you don't follow *my rules*, you burn for eternity."

I feel that it's important here for me to be clear that I'm not singling out Christianity. Islam says it also. So does just about every organized religion ever. They all have some version of "do what I say or there are eternal consequences waiting for you in a very bad place."

I think that's why many of us wander. We want to trust that our fellow man didn't twist the words of whatever gospel or religious text for his own purposes, but life has taught us different. Everybody's out to get their own. So, we're afraid to commit to a particular religion because they all say they're the only "right" one, and everyone else is wrong and going to burn for eternity. Who wants to burn for eternity because they believed the wrong person? Better to ride the spiritual fence and see who's standing after they all slug it out and decide.

We wander because we've become a society of spiritual fence-sitters. I was no different. I don't like being scared for a few seconds. Forget being scared for eternity. Easier to believe they're all out for their own ends and seek my own path.

I found myself in college, working like crazy on the start of the path to becoming a doctor. I was pre-med, a biochemistry major with an all too skeptical attitude. I was tired all the time, my senses toward the spiritual aspects of life reduced to almost nothing. I simply didn't have time for it. Still, I was wandering, and I knew it. I had no idea where to look for spiritual guidance, having burned a couple of bridges behind me already, and having no time to even read about anything but botany, chemistry, anatomy, and calculus. And because of my circumstances, being cut off from my spiritual self, I felt the need for spirituality all the more sharply.

What I needed was a strong connection. I needed a dramatic shift in my everyday paradigm. I needed a good story that I could relate to, to kick-start my spiritual journey.

So, I became an English major the next semester, where I could read and write as a major part of my education.

It was during that first semester in my new major, while I was searching for a story to connect with on a personal level, that I met my first pagan. We became fast friends, mostly because we were both musicians and writers, and our religions never really came up. He was a good friend, and I grew to trust him as much as I had ever trusted anyone. We became roommates the very next semester, and had an apartment to ourselves. We talked a few times about his religion (remember, I was still at least proclaiming to be a Christian), and I found it fascinating...but I noticed that there wasn't much he would ever say about the pantheon. It was all about the other guys in his group, and the things they did. They held feasts out in the woods, and drank beer out of horns, and acted like Vikings. It was intriguing, and it fit right in with my current search for the dramatic. I was hooked.

When his "clan" came over to the apartment one night to pick him up for a feast, I got to meet them, and they invited me along. We listened to death metal, and black metal, and drank beer from horns, and did a few little "rituals" out at their spot in the woods. They told me a little about the gods. They told me their version of history. I went home and came to the next morning with a hell of a hangover, but a great sense of satisfaction. They had invited me back, and it felt great to have friends.

For the next few months, I hung out with these guys. They made me feel important, like I was one of them. It was the first time in my life, even in family life, where I felt a measure of true acceptance. I felt a slight but rapidly growing connection with the Divine, and it was enough to make me feel like I had finally found the path to true spiritual connection. These people were loyal to me, they were my brothers, and they would die for me – or next to me – if need be. They inducted me into the clan, and made me their bard, their sage. Finally, I could study the Nordic gods in a real context and it would mean something to me.

I never saw it coming, but I suppose I should have.

Religions are all about rules. And my family was very religious.

Time for a reality check.

I was only slightly hung over the morning my parents knocked on the door of my apartment on campus. I also wasn't alone; some of the crew had stayed over that night after we got a little crazy and drunk. One of them wasn't even a member of the clan, just a friend of ours that we met at school who hung out with us occasionally.

He left while my parents stood outside waiting for me to dress and get everybody out of the apartment, so they saw which car was his. Remember that old joke thing people do sometimes when a car is really dirty, where they scribe something in the dust like "wash me?" We lived in a very conservative – and very Christian – town, so one of our group's members took it upon himself to spin that joke sideways by drawing a pentagram on the back windshield of this friend's car, with an inscription of "wash me...in blood!" in big letters. It was supposed to be funny for its sheer shock value, because this friend was very fond of driving around with very loud death metal blasting from his tiny, faded-red (almost pink) Dodge Neon. I mean, come on: death metal blaring from a pink Neon with a dusty pentagram on the back windshield and a stuffed animal hanging from a hangman's noose on the rearview mirror? That's hilarious. A little in-your-face avante guarde, maybe...but hilarious.

My parents didn't think it was funny. They accused me of falling in with a "bad crowd" and turning to devil worship, and promptly yanked their financial support, which forced me to move home. Don't get me wrong – they didn't pay for my school even as much as I did. I had student loans and two jobs to stay in that school, but without their piece I could no longer afford it. So, effectively, I was forced to move home and attend a different school that didn't cost nearly as much.

I moved home and switched schools like they wanted, but I didn't stop hanging out with my clan or listening to black metal or learning about the gods. You can imagine the circumstances. My parents made me come home so they could guide me back to the "right" religion by controlling everything they could. My music? Devil music. My books? Clearly, they were instruction manuals for devil worship. My choice in fashion trends? Obviously uniforms for summoning demons. To clarify: I was mostly listening to Rage Against the Machine and reading books about the Norse pantheon while wearing black jeans and black shirts. It's not like I was wearing a Halloween costume and corpse paint around town while blaring death metal and reciting incantations.

To be fair, we can't really blame our parents for the restrictions they place upon us. There is no how-to manual for raising children, and most parents do as they think best to keep us safe and healthy and on the "right" path. It's not their fault that they seem so imposing sometimes, not really. They're raised in a given faith, and they want their children to follow in their footsteps. Another spiritual path is completely alien, and maybe even dangerous, to their way of thinking. Even though I knew this, I still couldn't bear what they were doing, how they were treating me like a child. So, true to childish form, I felt that a little bit of rebellion was in order.

One day I came home from school and work, having been fired from my job for being late one too many times. My dad came home and saw me there, and was immediately furious. It didn't matter that I was late to work because I was in class at the school where he put me, or that the job was a dinky fast-food gig and I could have another one just like it the very next day. He laid down an ultimatum that I was to get my job back, whatever it took, before he came back in a few hours, "or else." We almost came to fists. I was scared, and emotionally hurt, and furious at the whole situation.

When he left to return to work, I saw my opportunity. I made a decision that would change my life forever.

If my family couldn't accept my new-found spiritual path, then they couldn't accept me. I packed everything I owned into my small car and headed back to the town where I had found my clan, and where they waited for me to return to them. When I got to town, I sold or pawned most of my belongings, emptied my bank account, and became as invisible as I could possibly be. I didn't have enough money to get into my own place, so I called my friends, but there was nowhere for me to stay without making them violate the terms of their apartment leases and being fined or thrown out themselves. I was on my own, and dusk was already dulling the light of day, creeping up on me like a patient assassin. It was almost winter, and already cold, particularly at night.

What had I done? I briefly considered going back to my parents' house, but I felt that I couldn't really call that home anymore, and I was afraid of the blowback from my decision to leave – things would only be worse now. Going back would prove them right, and force me to abandon my chosen path. I had a few hundred dollars, but no job, no degree, and no place to stay. I had a car, but not a way to get more gas money or pay for insurance without a job. I had a car and a couple bags of clothes.

I drove to the state park on the outskirts of town, by the river. I found a very secluded place to park, and settled in for one of the loneliest, coldest, worst nights of my life, with only my convictions and re-grets for company.

Just like that, I was homeless.

# Chapter Three

How does one define "true hardship?"

Yesterday I'd been in a hard spot, but at least I had my own room, a family that I'm sure loved me, and all the hot food and cold drink I could want. I woke up the day after I left the only home I'd ever known, and the only family I had, in my little car somewhere in the back forty of a state park, shivering and freezing my balls off.

At first, I couldn't figure out why I was awake. The sun hadn't even broken the horizon yet – not that I could see it for all the trees around me – and I didn't have an alarm to wake me up. Next to my left ear came a sudden, sharp *tap-tap-tap* against the driver's side window and a wheezy "Hey, man, you dead in there?"

I turned my head toward the voice and opened one bleary eye. The face in the window was lined, dirty, and shaggy with a grizzled grey beard. A great mane of long grey hair, looking like some electrical experiment had gone awry, framed the face of a man-hawk. A few colorful bruises and veins a little too dark marred the hard visage before me, almost invisible behind the patina of filth that came from living on the streets. Apparently, this is what I had to look forward to, now that I'd completely screwed the pooch. I met the man's only eye – the other one was covered by a bandana that was tied around his head – and received a startling jolt. *Oh, shit!* My brain was starting to come back to full function, and I realized he was talking to me.

"I said, you dead in there?"

I found my voice as I was struggling to get the car seat upright again, and myself along with it. I spoke through the window at the scary figure on the other side; to hell with giving that guy physical access to me. "No, I'm good. Sorry, just fell asleep."

He grunted, squinting at me. "Rough night, eh?"

"Yeah, something like that. Rough few months, actually." I squinted back. "Something I can do for you?"

"Yeah," he replied. "You're in my spot."

"Your spot?" I glanced around conspicuously. "It's a state park."

"Right. It's also my damn bedroom." He raised his eyebrows and pointed toward the rear of the car, where I had backed up against a low stone bluff the night before. The expression looked a little strange on him, what with the dirty bandana obscuring one eye.

I stared blankly for a second. "I don't get it."

"My bedroom!" he all but shouted through the car window, gesturing to the back of the car. "I had to crawl out of it under your car, and I forgot my bag. I got places to be today. Can you move?"

Another couple of seconds passed under my blank stare. *What the fuck is this guy playing at?* Then it struck me like ice water to the face: the state park was one place around town where the homeless bunked – one reason I had come here, since I was effectively now one of them. This was a homeless person, and I probably was really parked where he slept last night. Oops.

"Yeah. Sure, buddy. Sorry about that." He nodded as I started the car and pulled forward a little bit under his wary eye. I saw him walk back toward the stone bluff in the rearview as I put the car in park and shut it off. If I was going to live in the park, I might as well take the time to learn some of the rules and the lay of the land. I got out, trying to not be too obvious about locking the door as I shut it.

The old man was living in a small natural cave in the rock face – more of an overhang, really – beneath the bole of a large oak tree. I watched him for a moment as he rummaged through a collection of detritus, shoving the occasional odd item into a worn canvas bag that was slung across his body. He stepped out from his cave, straightened, and looked over at me. When he saw I was watching him, and was finally outside the car, he came over and stopped a few feet away, his steely grey eye focused on mine.

"You need some help," he said. It wasn't a question.

"If you have the time," I replied. "I know you have places to go. Sorry I blocked your...bedroom."

He smiled at that, and it was only a little terrifying on that face. "You apologize a lot for a guy who hasn't done anything wrong," he stated. "Don't worry about that. It's not like I have a name plate...or a door to put one on."

I chuckled, and so did he.

"I was wondering..." I started.

He interrupted me. "If I could show you around, tell you the rules, and introduce you." Again, it wasn't a question. I nodded. "Sorry, kid. I'm just passing through."

I hoped my look of desperation didn't show too much as I glanced around. When I looked back to him, he was staring at me intently, appraising me with his one good eye. "I can tell you're new to this, and the others will know it too. That's a starting point. Don't let them see you bleed. Learn how to fit in quick, or somebody's gonna roll you in your sleep and take your stuff."

I tried to hide the fear, but I guess I wasn't quick enough. "I...okay, thanks," I said weakly.

"What are you looking for?" he asked.

"I'm sorry?"

"There you go apologizing again," he said. "That's a bad habit you should break soonest, boy. You haven't wronged anyone here." At my look of utter helplessness, he continued. "You don't come from rich folk, but you have your own car. You're young. You look like you're in pretty good shape. You're healthy. You're clean, probably took a bath last night. Had a hot meal in the last day or so, too. You've got more clothes in your car than you can wear in a week, and even what you're wearing now is clean and could pass for respectable in most places. I see a suit hanging in your back seat." He paused, staring at me, waiting for a reply. I couldn't think of anything to say, so I just shook my head and stared at the ground. This guy wouldn't understand.

"You don't belong here," he said. The words stung more than I expected. I was an outcast even among the homeless. When I didn't say anything, he continued.

"You think I don't know? I've met a thousand kids like you. You're here by choice. You're looking for something. And until you figure out what that something is, here you'll stay."

I finally looked up at him again, my eyes stinging. I tried so hard not to let the tears start falling. I had made a choice to be independent, and it had cost me everything. This was all my doing. Only I was to blame for my current predicament.

"Listen," he went on, taking pity. "I know a guy who can show you around, show you the ropes. But you have to promise you'll listen to him. He doesn't have a lot of time to waste on charity cases, and he's not long on patience either." He appraised me with that creepy, cold gaze of his again. "You promise?"

"Yes, sir," I replied. "I promise."

He stared for a heartbeat more, intensely, and then nodded his head with a grunt. "We'll see," he said, and walked back to his little cave, where he snatched up a tall walking stick that leaned against the rock face. "I'll send him to you as soon as I see him again. Until then, learn how to fit in."

"I don't know how," I said.

"Sure you do," he replied. "When you go to a fancy dinner, do you wear only your dirty underwear and a top hat? Because that's what you look like now. You're in the middle of a bunch of homeless people, but you're wearing nice clothes and driving a nice car. Perhaps you should rethink your fashion sense, eh?"

I was shocked. I hadn't even considered that before.

"My point is, wherever you are, you should look like you belong there. Learn to blend in. Learn to fit in." He looked me over once again and barked out a sharp laugh. "Gluing feathers to your backside don't make you a chicken, boy."

I gave a nervous chuckle. *What the hell is he talking about?*

He started to walk away when I asked him "Where are you going?" I'm not sure why I asked that question; maybe I just didn't want to be alone. He turned and said over his shoulder, "Oh...I just *wander* here and there," with a glitter in his one cold eye. He continued, his voice low and quiet, "One more thing. Be careful who you follow around. Some people don't want you to see what they're hiding." He tapped the walking stick on the ground a couple of times, adjusting his grip, and started walking again.

"Where should I stay?" I called after him.

"You can have my cave," he said over his shoulder. "Looks like you'll fit in there, without all that baggage."

I watched him as he walked through the trees until I couldn't see him anymore, and wondered what the hell I was going to do now.

My first week as a homeless person was an intro-duction to true hardship, at least when compared to the rest of my life that came before. Your definition depends on your life experiences. My guess is that it's different for everybody.

All my friends were away with their families (or otherwise unavailable), so I was on my own. The would-be guide the grizzled man had promised to send my way hadn't showed, and probably never would. I mean, how would that person ever find me? It's not like he had even asked my name. No way, he wasn't coming.

I was alone, and cold, and utterly without hope. I found a place to park the car in an actual parking lot near the state park during the night, and made sure my few remaining belongings were hidden in the trunk, out of sight. I was at least smart enough to conserve what little money I had left to me and make a specific shopping list before I went on a spree.

I made two shopping trips. The first was to the local grocery store for a case of "just add water" noodles and other dry goods like a big bag of rice and a big bag of beans. My first day in the state park I saw a lot of people asking for money, for food, but they had been eating canned stuff in the morning and had the cans scattered around their campsites. I didn't know any of their names or anything about them, because they avoided me unless they were asking for money or food, but I watched them, and learned a few things I didn't expect. Like the thing about dry goods versus canned stuff.

I figured a lot of people in my situation made that first mistake – they bought canned goods or ready-to-eat meals, stuff that was mostly water and didn't give much nutrition or sustenance, and were therefore always hungry – and just kept doing it because they didn't realize that choosing convenience was a mistake. So, I went with dry goods that required a fire and time to cook. Considering my current situation, I could stand to eat rice and beans and noodles for a while. It seemed like a logical choice.

The second trip was to a military surplus store, where I purchased a small mess kit, a fire starter tool, a pair of tent halves, and a sleeping bag, the kind with the piece that cinches up around your head so you can withstand really cold temperatures. For those not familiar with tent halves, they are what the military issues to soldiers in the field as part of their standard mission gear. Each soldier carries half a tent that folds and rolls up nicely, and when it's time to set camp you can just snap the two halves together to make a whole tent and stake it down with a couple poles in the middle.

I swapped out my nice jeans and sweater for some old work jeans I'd held onto for several years with pajama pants underneath, a worn-out tee shirt layered over a long-sleeve thermal shirt, and old work boots. Now I looked like I pretty much belonged in the park among the homeless, I had shelter and food, and there was a river right next to me, so I could boil water to drink. I was smart enough to cover my basics, and I considered it a victory.

I wasn't smart enough to get a tarp, though. It rained my second night in the park. Since I had parked the car in a lot rather than keeping it with me, I didn't have access to a dry place except the cave, and it was small...and if I left the cave, I could be damned sure someone else would take it, along with the daily store of food and water and gear I'd cached. So, I sat in my cold little cave under the oak tree, shivering and watching the rain fall in sheets. I was too cold to sleep, and too lonely. As I watched the rain, I could swear I saw a bird staring at me through the curtains of water: a great black bird, perched on a low branch of a large oak tree. It was creepy in its intensity, but I shrugged it off, ignored it. I was too focused on my own fear and misery to notice. I missed my friends. I missed my warm bed back home, and I missed mom's meatloaf. Most of all, I missed my family. I folded in on myself and wept silently, cursing my decision-making paradigm while trying to convince myself I was right in what I had done.

I ended up crying silently in my cold, wet little cave most of the night, feeling sorry for myself while that big creepy-ass bird stared at me.

# Chapter Four

My third day in the park, the homeless started talking to me. I hadn't figured out my next move yet, and I didn't have anything else to do, so I talked back. I visited their camps, and listened to their stories.

Let me tell you: they were all sad stories. Not one person was there because they wanted to be there.

It was a sort of distant acceptance, them finally talking to me, and it was very strange. They were all friendly in their way, but nobody seemed to know anybody else very well, beyond where they slept. Nobody asked my name, and I didn't ask theirs. I just listened. They knew a lot about how to survive on the streets, and they gave me some good advice.

As I walked back to my meager camp, I thought about what I'd heard that day. There was one commonality between all of those stories, other than being sad. All of them had made a choice that had landed them in this park. Some of them had chosen drugs or alcohol over job or family. Some of them had chosen to commit a crime, and couldn't recover afterwards.

I had chosen to follow a path my family couldn't understand or accept. I had chosen to be militant and throw my spirituality in my parents' faces rather than just keep it quiet and personal. I had chosen my friends over my family.

Every single one of us had made a choice. I had chosen this.

"What am I doing here?" I asked myself quietly as I walked through the sparse woods.

A loud flapping noise shocked me out of my reverie, and I whipped my head toward the sound. A giant black bird was flying away, flapping its way through the lower branches, making a low *gruk-gruk-gruk* sound as it went. I must have startled the bird as I walked on this little path. I'd never seen a bird like that around here before, but I'd seen pictures, and read about them. It was the same bird that had been watching me last night, I was sure of it.

Was that a raven?

Nah, couldn't be. What the hell was a raven doing in central Texas? Did it escape from a zoo or something?

I shook my head and chuckled at the absurdity of this whole situation. I had to. It was either that or break down again, and I was fresh out of tears for the time being. Twilight was upon the park, and it would soon be full dark. The sky was clear, which was good and bad. Good in that it wouldn't rain again tonight, so at least I could get some rest. Bad in that it would be so cold I might actually freeze to death if I wasn't well-fed and tucked into my sleeping bag next to a small fire. I walked the mile or so to my car to make sure everything was alright and gather some food for a meal, then trekked back to my little cave.

I was correct in my initial identification. That *was* a raven. It was sitting in the oak tree over my earthen home when I got there, just staring at me.

Like I said. Creepy.

❦❦❦❦❦ ❦❦❦❦❦

Sure enough, it was very cold that night. I built a small fire to one side of my cave's entrance, and bundled up in my warmest coat and gloves. In the quiet, time seemed to stretch on and on, leaving me with my thoughts and the tiny meal I was preparing: rice and beans, again. I had traded a lady in the park some rice for a half link of dried smoked sausage, so that was in the pot, too. Despite eating the same thing for every meal, it smelled great hanging in the still, icy air, especially with the sausage adding its salty, smoky, savory flavor to the mix.

I was sitting at the front of a shallow natural cave on a blanket in the mud, lonely as all hell and wondering why I was living homeless in a state park, but the smell of food and the crackle of the warm fire helped my fear and anguish fade a bit. Celebrating the little things is important, I suppose. Especially when you have nothing else.

Again, I asked myself out loud, albeit quietly, "What am I doing here?"

A grating, gravelly voice answered me from the darkness. "Seeking."

I just about shit myself.

You'd be surprised how much privacy you get in a state park with other homeless people. There aren't any walls, but people give each other space and act like they don't hear you crying or muttering to yourself at night. Everybody does it, and everybody ignores it, like one of the many unspoken rules of being homeless. Nobody ever intrudes to the point of answering unless they think you're about to off yourself or somebody else they've come to care about. Even then, sometimes they don't intrude.

So, who the fuck just answered my question? I reached down to my boot as I stood, and silently withdrew a fixed-blade hunting knife from the sheath I kept hidden under my jeans. I glanced around through the darkness in the trees, careful not to let the firelight blind me. The razor's edge of the hunting knife gleamed. Nothing moved out in the night that I could detect.

There came a scratching noise, like small claws on tree bark. I stood stock still, waiting for an attack that might come at any moment, trembling. Then, an otherworldly clicking noise sounded in the night. It was coming from above me. I relaxed a little. It was just that damned bird.

A small *plop!* came from the ground next to my right foot, and I looked down to see an acorn in the mud. Well, I did live directly underneath a giant oak tree. At least no mud had splashed into my dinner.

But who had answered my question?

"Who's out there?" I asked in a stage whisper, trying to not wake up the rest of the neighborhood, just in case I was really going crazy. No response, and I still didn't see anything moving out there, and no other campfires either. Then that raven started *gruk-gruk-gruk*ing. I took a long, slow deep breath, and sighed heavily, expelling my anxiety and tension. Maybe it had been one of the other people in the park just screwing with me. Being homeless could get boring. The voice had sounded like a really raw *Slingblade* impression, after all. It had too much treble to it though, and not enough bass and phlegm. I sat down again and put the knife on the blanket next to me, just in case.

Time to eat. I picked up the little pot from the fire and opened my "hobo tool" (a multi-utensil like a pocket knife that had fork, knife, spoon, and can opener instead). Just before I put the first bite in my mouth, the raven landed in the mud on the other side of the fire. The spoon stopped in mid-air, savory goodness making my stomach twist in hunger, my mouth open and waiting.

*Check out the balls on this thing. Really?*

It's possible this raven had been hanging around the park for a while and had gotten used to people feeding it. I had noticed that some of the park's other inhabitants kept "pets." Maybe this was one of them, and it was hungry. Might as well be a good host. Maybe a little food would make this raven sleepy so it would stop making noise and I could sleep tonight. I put down one of the metal coffee mugs that came with my mess kit and doled in a dollop of my dinner.

The raven cocked its head both ways, staring at me, and puffed its feathers out. It hopped around the cup for a moment, *gruk-gruk-gruk*ing, and then started to eat.

I chuckled and spread my arms, one holding the pot of food and the other holding my hobo tool. "Hails, good raven," I said. "Be welcome to my hall."

My heart stopped in my chest and my blood turned to ice water when the raven answered me in that gravelly voice I'd heard a minute before.

# Chapter Five

"My thanks," said the raven.

I just stared in disbelief. *Fuck me. I am going crazy!*

"Correction," the raven replied. "You have been crazy for a long time, but not in the way that you think."

*You can hear my thoughts?*

"Yes." The raven pecked at the cup of rice and beans with its sharp beak, then took a drink from a mud puddle next to him.

"Uh. Okay." I didn't have anything better to say, so I just sat there staring at him. "What's your name?"

"What are yours?" The raven cocked its head sideways at me inquiringly. Creepy.

"I'm not sure I'm comfortable sharing that with a raven," I said.

"Because you do not yet know your names."

"Uh, yes I do. My name is…wait. Why did you say 'names'? I only have one." That sounded a little lame after it came out.

"No, you do not."

I didn't know what to say to that. Snarky little bird. "Do too."

"Do not."

It struck me then that I was arguing with a raven. The thought was so ludicrous I almost belted out a crazy laugh, which would have been all too appropriate considering how balls-out crazy this was. What the hell was going on? Nothing to do but roll with it, I decided.

"In point of fact, right now you have many names." He turned his head sideways to me, first one way and then another, so that at any given time he had only one black eye focused intently on me. I must say: little bird or not, that was pretty terrifying. The raven decided to prove me wrong. "Three that were given to you on the day of your birth. Two given by your friends. Two more given by your family. Many you have given yourself over the years in times of victory or defeat. Many more given by your former mates. Shall I continue?"

"Okay, I get it. I just never considered all those things my names before." I paused. "My ex-girlfriends? What did they call me?"

"I could tell you, but doing so would take more time than we have and none of those names would be good for your...confidence." I swear I saw a little twinkle in the raven's black eyes, and the beak parted slightly in what could only have been a grin.

"Very funny," I replied. "No thanks."

An awkward pause followed the brief exchange while I thought about all the things I'd been called over the years, the raven drinking water and eating food and giving me that same snarky little gaze. I decided to break it.

"Well, you obviously have me at a disadvantage. You know a lot about me, it seems."

"I do." The raven dropped the funny expression and cocked its head to one side. "You know more about yourself than you suspect, but you have forgotten. You may ask my name, if you wish...but I will not give it. Not yet."

That took me aback. "May I ask why not?"

"Names have power. You do not yet know how to respect and properly wield that power."

I considered that for a moment, and nodded slowly. "I can understand that."

The raven ducked his head once, and pecked another bean from his cup. "Now that I am your guide you will have no need to call upon me. When you need me, I will present myself. If you want to refer to me, or address me, you may call me 'raven' or 'guide.'"

"Guide?" I inquired.

"I was sent to guide you," he answered.

"By who?"

His voice grew somehow grave and serious. "My Master, Protector, and Friend."

Something tickled the back of my mind, a memory of ravens from my reading. I had read somewhere that they were considered messengers, guides, and teachers by the Old Norse. Odin had two ravens that brought him news of the nine worlds, according to the folklore.

Could this be...?

"Silence," said the raven. "Patience. You will come to know him in time."

I wasn't about to argue with a talking raven that was possibly sent here by Odin himself. I kept my teeth together and nodded, with a great deal more respect than before. Better safe than sorry. Besides, if it turned out I *was* crazy, at least I would have a decent excuse for my poor decisions.

The raven stared at me for what seemed like a long time, and I averted my eyes, looking to the small fire between us instead. "I was sent to guide you because you are seeking something."

"Seeking..." The single word that had answered my question a few minutes ago.

"Yes," said the raven. He peered at me and puffed his feathers again, making that eerie clicking sound only ravens can make. "You are here because you made a choice. You are seeking something."

"I haven't figured out what it is yet," I said, disappointment and frustration obvious in my voice.

"What do you lack?" asked the raven.

"A lot of things," I answered honestly. "Wisdom. Truth. Strength. Knowledge." I couldn't get the last word out, it tasted so bitter in my mouth and felt so distant and unattainable.

"Salvation," came the raven's quiet, rasping voice.

"Perhaps."

"That is a hard thing to achieve, for one who does not believe himself worthy."

The old weight I had felt my entire life settled even heavier onto my shoulders at those words. They were the truth, and truth could be a hard thing to bear.

"Why seek Truth if you cannot accept it?" asked the raven.

I looked up to see him peering at me with a strange expression for a bird: appraising, inquisitive, and knowing all at the same time. I didn't quite know how to answer, but I tried my best anyway. For the first time in a long time, I spoke straight from my heart.

"Because I know that I am weak. I haven't even the strength to face myself, let alone the many obstacles I face now and in a future I cannot know. Because I must face my demons if I am to learn and grow strong enough to survive this world. I feel that there is more to life than hiding and subsisting, and I will never find it – or my own worth – unless I know myself and my own strengths. I must become more than I am. I must find the missing pieces of myself."

My own candor surprised me, and I fell silent. I looked up to find the raven with an eager stance now, looking like it might start hopping in agitation at any moment. It had moved closer to me, and its voice came out quiet and grave as its eyes bored into mine. "A message I have for you," said the raven. I got an eerie, tense feeling that something tremendously important was about to happen, a gut feeling like standing at the very edge of a high precipice, about to fall. "A song shall I sing, if you will permit me, of the Path that you walk and the ways it is followed."

I kept my tense silence for a moment as I stared at the inscrutable bird before me. Then I nodded and said, "Sing me your song, good raven."

The raven waddled to the other side of the small fire again, and settled himself upon a stone facing me.

"First know that another choice you must make, before you continue this path," said the raven.

"Another choice?" I asked. The raven was sly, and would most likely do me no boon.

"A choice of the heart,

Mind, body, and soul;

You to this Path must commit.

It is rough, it is tough,

It is cold and alone,

And the Darkness is like a great pit.

Only one who can see

With more than his eyes,

And hear with more than his ears,

Will know when to run,

Will know when to fight,

Will know how to shed all his fears.

He will bleed, he will mourn,

He will stumble and Fall,

The One who chooses this Path;

In the end, it will make him

Feel more than alive,

For the Gods will Bless him with Wrath;

A new Life will he find,

When no longer is Blind,

And realize that he can,

With the help of no other,

No Mother, no Brother,

Change himself into a new Man;

But an Oath you must take,

And must never break,

As much to your Self as the Gods:

To Live, and to Learn,

And to never turn back,

And to struggle against all the odds."

I sat shocked for several long minutes while the fire crackled and popped between us. My gut feeling redoubled. Wasn't this the same kind of choice I had made just a few months ago that had landed me here in this cold, damp little cave? The only difference was that now it was for real. I could make all the oaths I wanted, standing in front of a mirror or in front of the other guys in the clan, or out in the woods by myself – those could fade and lose meaning, over time. This time, it was pretty clear that somebody with one hell of an awesome pet raven wanted my oath...and he wanted me to give it to myself.

I considered it again. I knew what I wanted, why I had come to this park. Why I had made those innocuous little choices to befriend certain people while alienating others. Why I had made the choice to leave my home and my family and live in a fucking cave. I needed to grow up, to find myself and my own personal strength. I was seeking myself. And if I ever wanted to find myself, I had to dig deep. A promise to myself that I would persevere, because if I didn't I would never forgive myself, never find my own strength, never find wisdom...and never find salvation. So, I gave my oath. The next seven words would change the course of my life in ways I could not yet fathom.

"No matter the cost, I stand fast."

"Very well," said the raven. He gave a loud, clear *caw*, and took wing into the cold, clear night.

# Chapter Six

I jerked awake leaning against the side of the tiny cave. The sun was just about to break the horizon, and my fire had gone out hours ago. I took quick stock of myself and my belongings, and sighed in relief.

It had only been a dream. A profound, informative, and life-altering dream that had turned my perceptions up on their ears, but a dream nonetheless. At least now I had some idea what I was doing out here beside my own foolish pride and lack of forethought. Now I could start pulling myself together and figuring out how to get out of this mess and back to my life.

I started gathering my gear, cleaning it and packing it away neatly in my backpack for transport back to the trunk of the car.

That's when I saw the little metal coffee cup sitting on the other side of the fire. *No way.*

I walked a few steps out from the cave and turned around to look up at the towering oak tree's canopy. For just a few moments, I thought I was in the clear. Then, just as I was turning my eyes back to the cave, I caught it in my peripheral vision and snapped my eyes back to the tree. There, on the left side of the trunk, on a low, thick branch, sat a raven. It was staring at me intently, just calmly sitting on its branch with its beak open in that same predatory grin it had shown me last night. Well, shit. Couldn't hurt to say hello to the raven, right? Just in case.

I gave a small salute to the raven and said, "Good morning." The raven didn't reply, just sat there with that ridiculous "I know something funny you don't" look.

"Who you talking to?" came a woman's voice from my left side. It was a lady who lived in the park, the one I'd traded for the sausage, walking out to panhandle for the day. I jumped just a little – I swear, just a tiny little bit – and oriented on her. She was peering at me through one wide eye, the other wincing against the bright sunrise.

"Uh...nobody. I was just saying it's a good morning, you know? Trying to be positive." I tried to look composed and definitely not like I'd almost shit my pants in surprise. It probably worked.

The raven started doing that weird clicking noise just then and – I shit you not – hopping foot to foot on its branch. Was that fucker laughing at me?

She appraised me seriously for another moment, and then said, "Don't go cracking up in the brain, now. Last guy did that got put in the nuthouse, and all the others took his stuff." She peered harder. "You're *not* going crazy...are you?"

"No, ma'am. Absolutely not. I'm solid." Yeah, right – and I was talking to a snarky raven last night that just made a joke at my expense.

She grunted in a knowing kind of way, and then continued about her business.

I glared at the raven for a moment, then nodded as if to say "Okay, nice one," and reentered the cave. A few minutes later, the last of my gear was packed in my bag. I slung it over my shoulders, cinched the carrying straps tight, and started hiking to my car.

One of my friends, the leader of our group, returned to town that afternoon. I went to his house, out in the country, where we usually held our feasts and rituals. I told him all about what had happened, and my current situation, and asked if I could stay with him until I was on my feet and had my own place.

He declined my request. He apologized, but it seemed feigned. He said it was up to me to make my own way, and he couldn't afford to help me, as much for my own good as anything else. I didn't expect that. I thought we were brothers, that we would do anything for each other. I took it a little hard, but I could see his point. I left his house and went looking for work, so I could start digging myself out of this mess.

I found a job that evening at a local restaurant where another member of our group worked. I was now a fry cook, making minimum wage. I was relieved that I could now buy more food; my finances had been running low already after the two shopping trips I'd made that first day. In addition, I got a discount on food from the restaurant. I started work right away, and didn't get out until well past midnight. I bought a small meal with some of my very little remaining funds to eat in the park. I drove to my parking spot, changed out of my work clothes and back into my regular outfit – which was getting quite gamey by now – and walked to my cave in the park. By the time I got there, I was exhausted. I put down my backpack, sat and leaned against my bedroll, and began to eat.

Just like magic, there he was. The raven waddled up to me and cocked his head sideways. He looked at me, then at my small plate of hot food, and then back to me. "I'm starting to think you're only in this for the food," I said, tearing off the lid of the to-go container and forking some of my food into it for him, then setting it down before him.

He ducked his head once in gratitude, then began pecking at the morsels in the lid. "Ridiculous," he replied. "I am also here for the women and laughter." He peered at me in an uncanny impression of the lady from this morning, and I broke out laughing. He did that clicking noise again, hopping from one foot to the other.

"You've got a great sense of humor, for a raven," I observed.

"Really? How many ravens do you know?"

Open mouth, insert foot. "Well...just you, so far."

"Wait until you meet my brother," said the raven. "He is hilarious. Or he thinks he is."

I chuckled a little at that, until I remembered my own little brother I had left behind to wonder what had happened to me. I thought of my mother, and my sister, and my stepfather, probably very upset and thinking me lost to them. For the time being, they were right. My parents were probably fighting about it right now. My mood deflated, and my appetite turned sour. I glanced to the side and saw the raven watching me.

"Painful, is it not?" asked the raven.

I furrowed my brow to show that I didn't catch his meaning.

"To remember the choices you have made, and how they have affected those you hold dear."

Oh, right. The raven could read my thoughts. I felt my eyes tearing up and averted my gaze. "Yes, it is."

"A good reason, then, to be more careful with your choices."

I nodded. "Yes. I still feel that I made the right choice, but it hurts. It hurts me deeply."

"The right choices sometimes do," said the raven. We finished our food in silence, and I cleared the mess, taking the trash to one of the bins along the park's trails. When I returned, the raven was sitting upon his stone again, staring at the ashes of last night's fire.

It was already bitterly cold, so I started another small fire to keep me through the night. When it was crackling merrily, I leaned back against the wall of the cave and said, "I wish I could see them right now, and let them know that I'm okay, and that I'm sorry for how I left."

"Your family miss you, and feel the same regrets as you. Your brother does not understand, nor your sister, but they still love you and pray that you are okay. Your mother prays also, and believes that you will one day find your way back home."

I stared at the raven. "You've seen my family?"

"Of course I have, many times. I am your guide along this path. How may I guide you if I cannot give you information?"

A million burning questions bubbled to the surface, but I swallowed them down. I could not ask the raven to send word to my family, any more than I could call them myself. To call them so soon, I felt, would invalidate my leaving in the first place – and then all this pain would be for nothing. I shook myself, wiping the tears from my cheeks, and stared at the fire.

After a time, the raven startled me out of my remi-niscence by asking, "What do you see?"

I looked out into the darkness. Nothing stirred ex-cept the branches of the trees and the grasses on the ground, and the leaves still blanketing the floor of the wooded area. I turned my head back to the raven. "Nothing out there I can see."

"Not yet," the raven replied. "I did not mean out there. I meant in the fire."

"Well...it's a fire. It's pretty, and hot."

"Clear your mind," said the raven. "What do you know of fire?"

"Probably too much," I said honestly. At least that's how I felt about it. "Academically, I know that it's a chemical reaction. I know how to start one, and how to put one out. I got burned a few times when I was younger." I paused. "Why? What should I know about fire?"

"Fire can be a great ally," the raven muttered, staring at the flames. "It cooks your food. Warms your body. Keeps danger at bay. Shows you safely through the darkness." He paused, and looked up at me. "Close your eyes, and tell me what you hear."

I shut my eyelids and listened to the fire. At first, I heard only the normal crackling and popping sounds everyone associates with fire. As I relaxed and focused on the fire, more sounds came to the foreground. "A low sizzling, like whispers from the base of the fire. High-pitched whimpers and wails, and screams from somewhere within. A constant dull roar, like a great wind."

"Yes," said the raven. "The voices are provocative, aren't they?"

"Yes."

"What do you feel?" he asked.

"I feel...." I tilted my head back, exposing my neck. I could feel the heat of the small fire warming the exposed skin, almost to the point of a burn. It gave me an itching sensation everywhere the warmth touched me. It was both comfortable and agitating at the same time. "I feel heat, almost searing me. Making me itch, but also helping me fight the night's chill."

The raven made a different clicking noise. "It drives you."

The simple statement made me open my eyes. "Drives me?"

"Yes. It is the fire inside you. The whispers of desire. The wails of despair. The screams of frustration. The roar of defiance. The warmth, a promise of what you lack. The burn, a warning of failure. The itch, a drive to seek what you desire. Do you see?"

The revelation shocked me to my core. This was something so simple, yet so profound. The fire was a representation of what lie within me. "I see," I replied. "Are all things like this?"

The raven stared at me silently for a few moments, considering something. He cocked his head to one side, and I got the distinct impression that he was listening to something I could not hear. Then he looked to the darkness outside the cave. "Not all things," he said. "It is enough that you now know a new way to view your world." He continued staring into the darkness around us, his eyes shifting and his head swiveling as if looking for something. He was behaving as if he sensed a threat. It put me on edge. I looked out to the same darkness, but did not see or hear anything.

"Stay close to your fire, and remember what you have learned. The Darkness approaches, and it is insidious." He whipped his head around to stare directly into my eyes and spoke in a hard-edged, serious tone that I had not heard him use before. "Have a care who you follow."

My blood ran cold. The raven took flight, and was lost to the darkness outside the cave. I moved the fire into the center of the cave's entrance, and built it just a little higher before curling up against the back wall with my knife hidden in my fist inside the sleeping bag.

# Chapter Seven

I sat there, against the rocky back wall of the cave, and stared at the darkness outside. Why had the raven been so tense? Why had he warned me to stay close to the fire? I couldn't see or hear any threat out there, but he had acted as though we were being hunted, stalked by a lethal predator.

I looked up above the canopy of the trees, to the stars. After my revelation about the fire, I wondered about the stars.

Then, as I sat there being all deep and ponderous, I almost shit my pants again. A voice came from somewhere outside the cave. It was a deep, slippery whisper that slithered out of the darkness. It seemed to wrap me in the coils of a great serpent, and to invade my very being, enveloping me in a cold so deep and absolute I could hardly draw breath. I could not move. I could not even close my eyes. I could no longer see the fire.

I simply stared at nothingness, and felt it stare back...and I heard the Darkness speak to me.

*There is no Light*, said the Darkness. It was echoed by a thready chorus of other voices. *No Light!* they cried. *No Light!*

*There is no Light, aside the Light you've been taught to create in your own mind.*

I tried to cry out, to struggle against it, but found myself powerless.

*That pitiful spark must be extinguished*, continued the voice. *It must be snuffed from existence before the real training of your thoughts can begin. Learn to thrive in Darkness. Darkness is ancient. Darkness was here long before Light was conceived.*

I looked up. If only I could see the stars! I squinted, and struggled all the harder against the oppressive weight. I finally got enough control back to shout, "Not...true!"

The Darkness laughed, sounding for all my soul like a million snakes hissing and slithering and rattling. It felt like something slicing my insides apart with sharp shards of ice. *Has nobody told you?* the Darkness jeered. *The only Truth is a Truth that cannot be seen.*

My eyes felt like they were frosting over, and the world crystallized...and then shattered in a squeal and sharp crack like a rifle report. I slammed my eyelids shut in fear. The roar from the explosion filled my ears, but it didn't fade. I felt my limbs start to come back to me, and opened my eyes to find myself kneeling and stifled. The world had changed.

An endless sea of figures surrounded me on all sides. None of them had faces. They were all moaning and wailing and screaming and murmuring – it was maddening. I had a shield in my left hand, and they were pushing against it, against me, trying to force me down and trample me underfoot. I pushed back, and after a great struggle, managed to stand upright. My limbs felt like they were all mired in thick mud, moving slowly and only with serious effort.

I stood in a deep valley. In front of me, a million miles away, I could see the moon – very faint – above a high ridge. I had to get there. I had to see the stars. I started pushing and shoving at the figures around me, frantically trying to force my way forward.

I pushed my way through that thronging sea for what seemed like several blended nights in a row. The Darkness was all around, consuming me. The ridge I was trying to reach was no nearer than it had been when I started. The Darkness grew more thick and infernal all around me, obscuring the figures that pressed in. I started to get confused. I was so tired. I could hardly move anymore. The world was growing darker everywhere, and the edges of my vision were blurring.

I screamed in frustration and pain...and heard my name whispered in that slithery, greasy, cold tone.

I started to feel more comfortable, to move more easily. The world grew darker by the moment now, increasingly black. Where was I going? Something about...stars, maybe? My name came from the inky black all around me now. The voices of the figures were starting to take on tone and cadence – they were chanting my name, in a thousand different ways. This Darkness was something alien, yes. But it was also familiar, somehow. This Darkness was something I knew.

*Let go of your shield*, it whispered to me. *Join us.*

"No," I struggled to say.

*All of your friends are here, waiting for you.* I looked around me. Some of the faces took on definition of a kind, but everything was so dark and blurry. I recognized friends long past, and not yet met. How could this be?

"No," I said again, more firmly. "It's a lie." I looked around for some way to see – a fire, a flashlight...something. Anything to give me some light.

*There is no Light, aside the Light you've been taught to create in your own mind*, reminded the Darkness. *Come and join us. What is it that you seek? Companionship? Riches? A battlefield to sate your hunger for violence? You will find it all with us, and so much more. There is no greater promise than the freedom we offer you.*

Then, very clearly, I heard the raven's words echo in my head. *Stay close to your fire...remember what you seek!* I did remember, then, what I was looking for: the stars. The moon above the ridge. I had to get there. I could do it.

Suddenly, a torch appeared in my right hand, smoldering with a dim light. The Darkness screamed in protest.

"Lies!" I shouted. "Empty promises!" Where was I going to find a damned light? All I wanted to do was return to my cave. Steeling myself, I turned in the direction I thought I had once seen the ridge, and the moon, and started pushing through the crowd again. Temptation had failed, so the Darkness turned to threats.

*It matters not. Your little light will die out soon enough.*

"I have my own Light," I replied in a growl. "My faith lights my way." The torch smoldered brighter, taking on small wisps of flame.

*You walk in Darkness. Blinding yourself with that Light is foolish. What if you stumble? Fall? Hurt yourself? Who will find you? Who will care for you?*

"Not foolish – brave. If I stumble, I will get up again. If I hurt myself, I will tend my own wounds. I need no other to care for me." The torch grew brighter.

*And if you get Lost? Shall your Spirit wander eternally in Darkness?*

"I will never be Lost, for I can find my own way. I need no guide, aside my faith." The torch took serious flame. I could almost see through the figures. I could faintly see the outline of the moon again, peeking out over that ridge. I was a little bit closer than I had been. I redoubled my efforts to push my way through the crowd, and started brandishing the torch at the figures who got too close.

*You will be cursed. You will be tortured. Your way will always be difficult.* The Darkness jeered at me, dripping with hatred and disgust.

"That is my choice, and I have made it. Though I face any curse, any torture, any foe, I shall endure, and I shall conquer. Though I face any obstacle, I shall overcome." A lance of agony stabbed through my head, and I staggered.

*You cannot overcome your Fate.*

"That may be true," I growled, "but my Fate is my own. The Well of my Faith is ever-deep, and will sustain me through all things."

*Then you deny the Darkness?*

"I deny it. Be gone, that I may seek my own way. The Light to seek my own path lies within me, and cannot be given by others. I command you...be gone!" A figure rushed out of the Darkness at me, and I reacted. I swung the torch as hard as I could at the figure as it flew toward my face.

"Aaugh!" I cried out as I jerked awake in the little cave, thrashing and brushing myself off. I scrambled to my feet – as much as I could, given the low ceiling – and looked around sharply. It was daylight, and I was alone.

Seriously: fuck all this insanity business. What the hell was happening to me?

I heard a flapping of wings, and the raven landed at the entrance of the cave, peering at me. I stared back at him, then took a quick look around to make sure nobody was watching or listening. The coast was as clear as it was ever going to be. In my best stage whisper, I said, "What's going on?" I was still shaking from the adrenaline of the intense...nightmare? It had been a nightmare, right?

That raven cocked his head to the side. Then he looked at the head of a trail that led even deeper into the park. I got the message: *not here*. I got my gear together and stowed into my backpack, and the raven flew to the head of the trail, perching on a low branch. He made that *gruk-gruk-gruk* sound until I caught up, then he said quietly, "Follow me," and flew to another tree further down the trail. I did my best to walk normally, as though I were just a tourist, and followed the raven.

After about a mile, we were out of the park. After another mile, we were out and away from the city. Another mile later we couldn't hear the country highways or anything even related to civilization: like I said, small town. He led me to a secluded, thick copse of trees on the bank of the river. It was extremely quiet, except for the bubbling sounds of the water and a few small nature noises. The raven settled himself on the trunk of a fallen tree. I sat down on a boulder at the water's edge, and made with the questions.

"Okay, answer time. I'm freaking out. What the hell is going on? I mean, I'm talking to a raven, I'm dreaming but I'm not dreaming...I don't get it." The raven stayed silent for a moment more, cocking his head as though listening again. "A little help here?" I prompted.

"You're in the Mist," croaked the raven. He cocked his head again. Was he listening to something, or waiting for me to speak, or what? A minute went by without a sound before I spoke.

"The Mist," I said. "Okay, sure." I sighed heavily. "That...confused me even more."

The raven did that agitated clicking noise that only ravens can pull off, puffing his feathers. "The Mist, boy. The fog that obscures your vision and keeps you from seeing the other worlds."

I felt my jaw drop a little. "The, uh...*other* worlds? As in, *the Nine*?" No way, couldn't be.

Rather than answer, the raven asked another question. "What do you know of the Nine?"

"Not enough, apparently."

The raven said, "Wrong. Too much. You have too much false knowledge drawn from incorrect sources. We will not discuss the Nine for now. I am referring to the other worlds that exist inside you."

"Inside me," I said.

The raven got even more agitated and shook himself. "Remember the fire. What you seek is within you, not without. You said yourself that you know there is more, but you cannot see it. The Mist is what blinds you. It hides what you would not willingly see." He paused, as if deciding how much to tell me. "You built it to protect yourself, when you were very young."

I thought about that for a while, mulling it over in my mind, walking around the little clearing, staring at the water. The Mist could refer to how we blocked out bad memories and traumas from our past. Things we didn't want to see. Things we couldn't handle seeing.

"I think I understand. It's a wall of sorts that I've created in my mind."

"Yes," said the raven. "As you grew up and realized that your elders didn't see the things you did, it made you feel...different. You were told those things didn't exist, so you covered them in Mist. However, your mind knows those things exist, and the Mist can be treacherous. It fades, gives you small glimpses in times of heightened emotion."

"Like dreams and nightmares," I said, understanding a little more.

"Yes." The raven waddled to the shore, and drank from the river. "This is what happens when you see things in the shadows, or have dreams. The Mist is showing you something it thinks you want to see. You are seeking a missing piece of yourself, truly, and you have entered the Mist. You are piercing the Veil."

"That's crazy," I said. "You're saying my own mind is doing this to me?"

"Of course," replied the raven. "All realities – all worlds – are a matter of perception. Your mind interprets the world around you and within you, allowing you to perceive...well, I suppose you could say that you may see whatever you want to see." The raven turned away from me, waddling back to the fallen tree. "You asked for the truth, did you not?" He hopped up onto the tree trunk and turned to face me.

"Yes, I did." I sighed. "I guess I was just expecting something a little less dramatic than waking nightmares."

"Your ancestors learned to exist in all worlds," said the raven. "They saw the Mist manifested in the physical world, and learned to separate the worlds within from their waking reality."

"Great. You're saying I need to 'live in the now.'" I walked back to the bank of the river and stared at the water again. "What about this nightmare I had last night? What about the Darkness?"

"The Darkness lives within us all," replied the raven. "It is seductive, and easy to follow. It is the ultimate blindness to all else but what you wish to see. It is ultimately ruinous. You did well to resist it last night, but you are not out of the Darkness yet. That was only the first of many tests."

"Tests?"

"The knowledge you seek is dangerous. Those who have not been tested cannot be trusted to hold it." The raven looked at me sternly. "You chose to walk this path."

I felt a little ashamed for my complaining tone. "Of course. My apologies. I need guidance."

The raven was doing that listening thing again when I turned around to look at him. He saw me watching and stopped. "I have given you all the guidance I can, for now. You must find your own way through the Darkness." He spread his wings to take off, but I stepped forward suddenly as I had a small inkling of insight.

"Wait! I have one more question before you leave me."

The raven held his wings outstretched, and turned his head to me. I asked him, "In these nightmares, why do I want to see the stars so badly? The fire reflects my desire to change. What are the stars?"

I saw a twinkle of respect in the raven's black eyes, and he refolded his wings momentarily. "The stars are the souls of your ancestors: warriors and heroes; hunters, gatherers, and farmers; sons, fathers, and grandfathers. They are the line of your people. They are who came before. The knowledge, wisdom, and strength you seek – their legacy – lives in *you*." I gaped, knowing it was absolutely true. He paused just long enough to deliver a warning.

"Only those who have been tested, who have found themselves, can truly know their ancestors...but that does not mean that some who walk among you now cannot make up stories to twist your path and use your blindness against you, and against others." He spread his wings and leapt into the air, calling back to me, "Have a care who you follow."

Then he was gone.

# Chapter Eight

After the raven left, I took some time to reflect on and think about what I'd experienced, what I'd learned so far. I did not see the raven again during that time. I worked, and took long walks through the park, and survived. I did not hang out with the crew. I did not attend band practices. I didn't call anybody. Sometimes I thought about my family, and the still-fresh wound would tear at my insides. I had resolved not to contact them until I could return on my own terms. Going back before I got myself well and truly together would only bring back more of the same troubles that existed before I left...probably made all the worse by my failure.

I went back to my friends after a couple weeks and it was tricks as usual. Maybe just a touch more intense than before, since there now seemed to be a push to make ourselves known to everybody. There was more tension than normal between our band and others, our group and others. I hardly took notice. I was working hard on getting my shit together and getting out of the park. Still, when I had time, I relished hanging out with the crew I had now been part of for more than a year – that group of modern-day Vikings who made life so intense and interesting, whose leader knew so much about our people and where we came from. It was all about the dramatic draw of the distant past, for me: stories of a time when heroes truly walked the earth. I was in a bad place. I needed to believe that my ancestors were grandiose warriors and heroes all. Their heroism had built the modern world, after all, and had given us life. They had survived some serious shit, not all that different from what I was going through, and had even made the best of it. And after saving the world time and again, they had obviously all had a beer (or many) and a good laugh about the whole thing.

After several months at the restaurant, I finally caught a break. I landed a job at a newspaper, working as a section editor. It was right up my alley, and I loved the work. It also paid better than the restaurant, and after a few more months I had enough savings to get into my own apartment. It wasn't anything fancy, but it was finally a roof over my head, and it felt good to have some true privacy and *oh my goodness, hot water.*

I knew I was on the right path, deep down. I felt it in my bones. I just had to stick to it. And since I was so certain of my path, I felt certain that every other aspect of my life was proceeding according to plan, leading me to the right place.

Oh, how blind we can be when we mix religion and real life.

See, when you're on a quest to find the good in life, there's this ongoing theme that everything is all good, all the time, according to the stories you hear from others. All the bad parts are just glossed over or not mentioned. Also, it's all relative to the audience listening to the stories: it didn't really occur to me that the heroism of my ancestors did not make *me* a hero by default.

It also didn't occur to me – though I had been warned multiple times – that the people I trusted most would not only gloss over the bad, but also throw a whole lot of bullshit into the mix. I should have taken the raven's warnings literally. But, you know: youth and wisdom, etcetera.

I'll say this for our group: we were a hard-boiled bunch. A couple of them had rough childhoods or adolescence, sure, but it wasn't really about that. It was about showing the world what we were capable of. Some of us fought in the Society for Creative Anachronism, or SCA. If you're a fan of medieval times, I highly recommend you check them out – very cool hobby to have. We all worked hard. We played harder. And we were loyal to each other. We were brothers.

All of this – the attitudes, the backgrounds, the alienation from family and society, and most of all the sheer will to prove ourselves at *something* – added up to only one possible outcome.

We did some seriously crazy shit.

Let me be clear: none of it was illegal, not even in the slightest. It's just not stuff that sane people do. Even down to just walking around...you know, at night. With no moon. In the pitch black. *Toward* the sounds of wild boar. Slugging it out *Fight Club* style with each other over a beer. But, you know, with blunted swords, dressed in whatever armor we could find and strap on whilst mostly drunk. Getting hammered and then challenging one another to a footrace across a deep ravine and up a treacherous hill to the feasting area. Traipsing out into the wilderness for a long weekend with nothing but a knife to see if we could survive.

Good times.

Suddenly, things got scary. The talk gained a hard edge, and we were suddenly talking about things that would get us pinched and put in the pokey. I didn't like the sound of it, but at the time it was only talk – and I knew it. At least two other people in that group had way too much to lose by getting into trouble with the law, mostly because they were already on probation. I knew they wouldn't do those things...but they were talking about them. I smiled and nodded, and waited to see what would happen.

One night our band played a show in a big city a few hours' drive away. Of course, it was a bar, and it was night when we *started* playing, so it was nearly three in the morning before we started the drive home. Oh, yeah: and we were paid mostly in alcohol. All of us, and our equipment, were in an old, single-cab truck, which meant that two of us had to ride in the back. I pulled short straw on that one, along with one other guy.

We got in the bed of the truck and hunkered down as much as we could. At this time, it was winter again, and a wet one to boot. So: imagine huddling in the bed of a truck, staring out the back, in about 20-degree weather, while being shredded to ribbons with little sleet crystals slashing at your face, drunk. You have three hours – at least – before you're home, and you're freezing balls, and you have no coat or way to cover up, and you've already been sweating for three hours straight. Just trust me on this one: it sucks worst. That's the scene.

As you stare out the back of the pickup at the sleet flitting through the rear lights of the truck, the yellow lines start to move *away* from the driver's side of the truck. The truck starts to buck and jump as it hits gravel. You turn around and scream with what voice you have left that the cold hasn't already stolen, and pound on the back window of the truck's cab to wake up the drunk driver.

Imagine three hours of doing that shit over and over again, every fifteen minutes or so.

"We're gonna fucking die," said my friend.

"Yep," I agreed, teeth chattering. "Fuck it."

That's the attitude we had cultivated in our group. No fear of death. No fear of mutilation or dismemberment. If we got cut up and scarred, it would only make us more terrifying. We had even earned a reputation in the town where we lived. People avoided us like a living plague. We had *become* fear.

It was the warrior spirit, and it felt fucking great.

Still, that's when I got my first inkling that what we were doing was pure insanity. What the hell were we trying to prove, taking stupid risks like this? Why was I suddenly dressing in all black with tall boots and chains and such? Obviously, some of that was just because I was finally part of a group, and that's what we all did. But....

What were we fighting for?

The question got more complicated after a few more months. I was in a store one day, just shopping for groceries, when some corn-fed hillbilly beefcake came up to me out of nowhere and started threatening to kick my ass because I was friends with his girlfriend's ex-boyfriend. I don't scare easily, and when I do get scared, I get dangerous. It's just how I've always been. When I get really scared, it's because I think I'll probably die, or at least get into trouble serious enough that it's probably throwing away the rest of my life. Ever hear the turn of phrase "the only good snake is a dead snake?" Exactly. When I'm in fear for my life, in any respect, I go for the kill shot.

So, I started shaking like a leaf. The ex-boyfriend in question was our group's leader. Either I would remain loyal to him and sort this hillbilly out, or I would let it go and have my loyalty called into question. Rock, meet hard place.

It may have been my incessant shaking that tipped him off to the fact that I wasn't looking for a fight. He left, and I went home to think about what had happened. I couldn't relax, weirdly enough, because the post-conflict adrenaline had turned into anger and embarrassment. There was only one place I could ever really let go now.

I drove across town, parked the car in the lot I had found, and walked to the park.

# Chapter Nine

My little cave was occupied again. The old man with the grizzled grey hair was back, and he wasn't alone this time. He sat by a small cook fire at the entrance to the cave, stirring a small black cast-iron pot with a wooden spoon, and two hungry-looking pups lay beside him. I approached slowly, and let the man see me. He smiled, looking for all the world like a wolf in the know, and waved me over with his free hand.

When I got close enough, I went to shake his hand in greeting…and stopped dead when both pups lurched to their feet, hunched down as if ready to strike, and let out low warning growls. I backed off, slowly. The old man glanced at both pups in turn, and then grunted, giving me that appraising eye of his. I saw something there, but I wasn't sure what exactly. I felt like I was being measured, judged somehow. After a moment he grunted and looked away from me. "Seems like they smell something they don't like on you," he said. "I smell it, too. Smells like rot." His eye momentarily bored into mine, but he seemed to make up his mind about something. He grunted again and looked back to his cook pot.

That took me aback. I'd just had a nice hot shower in my attempts to calm my nerves. I took a quick sniff, just to be sure I'd put on clean clothes. Strange. I smelled like plenty of good soap.

"I'm sorry I disturbed you, sir," I said. "I'll leave you to your meal." I started to turn and walk away, but he stopped me with a bark-like laugh.

"I didn't say you," he chuckled. "Something on you. Doesn't matter right now." He gestured to the large stone across from him, where the raven had so often sat when I lived there. "Have a seat, boy, and be welcome. You hungry?"

Something not a lot of people know about being homeless: if a very poor person offers you food when they typically don't have any to spare, it's considered quite rude to refuse their offer. You would think it's the other way around, but it's not. Being refused when you're trying to give someone else all you've got – and you already have nothing – can really sting the feelings hard. It makes you feel even worse about your already bad position that people feel pity for you.

"I wouldn't mind a bite to eat," I said with a warm smile. "And as it happens, I've brought something to share also." I pulled from my pocket a small bottle of the best Scotch whiskey I could afford at the time.

The old man's face split in another wolfish grin, his eyes flashed, and he barked laughter again. "Well met, son!" he exclaimed. He pulled a small bowl from his bag and began filling it with what I assumed was stew. When he passed it to me, I tasted it. It was hot, and rich, and chased away the cold like a fire inside. It was the best thing I'd tasted in a long, long time.

"What is this stew? It's fantastic!" My belly growled for more. I hadn't eaten anything all day, not after the confrontation with the corn-fed hillbilly.

He gave me a secretive smile, as though letting me in on an inside joke. "Squirrel," he said with great relish and a little shiver of pleasure. "Been trying to catch that chattering little bastard a long time, and I finally got him. Tastes better than I ever imagined." His face drooped a little, and he huffed a quick sigh. "Course, there will be another one just like him tomorrow. Chattering away. Causing mischief." I swear, that knowing frown he put on made him look just like my Grandpa.

He stared at the fire, and so did I. We were quiet for a few minutes while we ate in silence. The fire, dancing and hissing and warm, seemed to calm me down far more than anything else that day. Or perhaps it was the stew. Or both.

I came back to myself and passed him the bottle of Scotch for the first pull, and took one myself after him. He eyed me again, only for a moment, and said in a pensive tone, "Something on your mind."

"Yeah," I agreed, noting again that he hadn't asked a question. Eerie. I felt the emotions roiling again, threatening to boil over as I prepared to launch into a tirade about the latest pile of crap in my life. "It just…." I paused. I didn't know this guy. He didn't know me. He was feeding me awesome stew around a warm campfire in what was his only semblance of a home. He had shown me true hospitality, in a way many people never really get to experience. I had absolutely no right to break the mood and unload my problems on him. Instead, I sighed and said, "It's nothing. Trying to figure out my life, and things keep getting in the way. Too much confusion, too much fighting with no victory."

He nodded as I spoke, staring at the fire.

"I'm disillusioned. I feel like I'm just spinning my wheels. I'll get over it." I hung my head when I finished, and took another pull from the bottle of Scotch.

Out of nowhere he asked, "What are you looking for? Seeking? Fighting for?"

My gaze snapped up to him, recognizing my own unspoken questions given voice by him. "Excuse me?"

"You're looking for something. I knew it the day I met you. You've gotten out of this park, obviously you're much better off than you were then. But you still haven't found what you're looking for." He looked directly at me again, and that eye locked gaze with my own. "What do you lack most? What is it that you want?"

I stared hard at him for several moments, my jaw clenched tight. My inner turmoil won the battle with my poker face and bubbled over, and I spoke. "I don't know anymore."

He looked back to the fire, and grunted. "A funny thing, fear," he said. "It can sneak up on you in a thousand different ways, drive you mad. Make you think you've beaten it, only to discover with your last breath that you've been carrying it with you the whole time." He gave me a sidelong glance. "It can rot you from the inside, and turn you into something you're not."

I looked from him to the fire again, and focused on the burning sensations on my face as I watched the flames dance. It burned my eyes, dried them out until I could hardly see. It seemed like several minutes went by before I spoke. The old man let me have my silence.

"You're saying my fear is blinding me."

"It blinds us all, at times," he said. "It whispers to us all the bad things it can conjure in our imaginations. Plays on what we value, those we love. Makes us think that if we're cautious enough, if we just play by the rules, we'll get to keep all those things, and everything will be okay." He paused and looked pointedly at me. "Trick is to realize that there's nothing you can do about all those bad things. What will be...*will be.*"

"Fate?"

"That doesn't matter so much, not to little ants like us. We're too tiny to even comprehend such things. Don't think on such a grand scale. Which would you rather do: live a full and happy life, free of the fetters of fear, making memories and being in the moment...or live a dull and fearful life, always shivering when you think of what might happen if you step outside for a walk? Whether your doom was preordained or not, you'll never know. All you can do is forge ahead and make the best of what you have been given."

I had never thought about it quite like that.

"You're walking in a warrior's boots, son," he said. "Probably because you think you lack courage or strength." When I opened my mouth, he held up a hand to stop me. "Anyone who has ever met you knows that you lack neither of those things. Nor do you lack patience, or will, or confidence, or even knowledge. You have wisdom beyond your years, though you don't always follow it."

I held my silence as he ate a little more stew and took another pull of the Scotch, clearly savoring its peaty, smoky essence. "Yet you are covered in fear." He looked pointedly at the pups, then at me. "We can smell it all over you."

"I have little to fear from anything anymore," I said. I didn't mean it to come out so harshly, but even I could hear the dripping derision in my voice. "I inspire fear."

"Wrong," said the old man, his lone eye tracking back to meet mine. "You fear yourself. You fear what you will become. You fear that you will never find salvation, though you don't know what that is. You fear that you will always be alone, left to wander through the Darkness without anyone to care for you or show you the way. You fear that your faith is misplaced no matter where you place it. You do not think yourself worthy of love or respect, and fear that you will never know them." His voice turned hard, and got very quiet. "You absolutely stink of fear. You just don't know it."

I got very angry then. I felt my face burn, and knew it was starting to color with rage. "What do you know about it?" I growled. Both pups immediately turned their heads toward me, and bubbling growls came from their throats as their eyes fixed on me.

"I know you're giving a lot of good people a bad name," he said, his voice clearly menacing. His upper lip twitched in that way that wolves do when they're baring their fangs. "I know you're needlessly harming more than just yourself." His voice grew even more quiet and intense. "I know you're following others down a ruinous path to a doom that isn't yours because you're too afraid to know yourself."

I leapt to my feet with a snarl and unleashed my pain in his direction in the form of a fighting stance. The pups snarled back and flashed their teeth for real. I didn't care. "You don't know me, old man!"

He stood up from his seat by the fire, slowly, walking stick in hand, and turned to me with his head hung like somebody defeated. I kept my stance and my snarling expression, ready for a fight, until he raised his head to look at me. I stared in shock, and felt the heat of the moment bleed out of me.

A single tear track ran from his lonely eye and down his cheek into his beard. He raised that eye to meet mine and said, "I know you better than you know yourself, son."

I didn't know what to say. Embarrassment replaced my anger. Maybe he saw something of himself in me, and was trying to warn me. "I don't know how, but okay," I replied. "I'm sorry I did that just now. I don't know why I lost my temper." He just nodded quietly. "Please keep the whiskey as a token of my apology, and thank you for the stew," I managed to get out. I was starting to tremble, and I didn't want him to see that.

"You are always welcome here, though I don't think we'll see each other again for some time. Take care of yourself," he said.

"You too," I said.

As I turned to walk away, I heard him say softly, "Have a care who you follow."

I spun around at hearing him speak the raven's words from several times before, but the old man and the pups were gone. Only a lonely little fire crackled and sputtered, burning low and dying out, at the mouth of the tiny cave.

I walked back to my car, and drove back to my apartment with even less peace of mind than I had started with.

# Chapter Ten

"Oof!"

I spun around and fell flat on my backside, spilling two paper bags of groceries out of my arms and all over the ground just outside the store's exit.

I looked up dazedly to see the brick shithouse I'd just walked into standing over me with a mildly confused and worried expression on his face. "You alright, buddy?", he asked. He extended a broad, beefy hand down to me in an offer of help in getting back to my feet.

I'm not *that* proud. I took it and let him help haul me up. I briefly dusted myself off and answered, "I'm okay. Sorry about that."

I looked him up and down quickly, sizing him up, just in case. The man was a beast: almost seven feet tall, broad-shouldered, with arms and legs like freaking tree trunks. He was dressed like a carpenter. When my eyes came back to his face, I saw friendly ice-blue eyes and a big, warm grin. His whole sun-drenched face was framed with a long mane of red hair and a red beard. His smile and the look in his eyes was a little too knowing, but not at all hostile...just ready. He'd noticed my size-up and had probably done the same thing. So, he could probably fight. Instead of starting trouble, though, he was holding out his hand to me again. "Entirely my fault," he said. "I take up a lot of room, and don't always mind my surroundings well."

I laughed, shook his hand, and gave him my name. "Perfectly fine," I said, and stooped to begin gathering my spilled groceries. To my surprise, he also squatted down and began helping me. "I'm sorry," I said again. "I didn't catch your name."

He squinted at me out of the corner of his eye and said, "Some call me...Tim?"

I barked out yet another laugh, and he chuckled. A fellow Monty Python fan. This guy could be a friend of mine. "Well met...Tim," I said.

He glanced over at me as he gathered and bagged my groceries. "Nice hammer," he said quietly.

I immediately stopped what I was doing, and my eyes snapped up to his. I just froze. It wasn't common, in that place, for anyone to notice my necklace pendant, since I typically kept it hidden under my shirt. It was even less common for anyone who did notice it to know that it was a representation of a hammer. Thor's hammer, to be precise.

"It's a bit stylized, for my tastes," he continued, "but I'd recognize Mjollnir anywhere." He reached up to the nape of his neck and tapped a simple brass hammer of his own.

"You know the Norse pantheon," I said in a hushed tone.

He chuckled softly. "I don't know about 'pantheon,'" he responded, "but yeah. I'm familiar."

I raised a single eyebrow, wondering what he'd meant by that, but no more was forthcoming. Strange. After a few more moments of gathering my scattered food items, we were done. We stood up, and I picked up the grocery bags again. "Thanks for helping me out," I said. Before I walked away, I had a peculiar urge and asked, "Can I buy you a cup of coffee, and pick your brain?"

He looked at me appraisingly, then nodded. "I'm busy this evening, visiting my dad. Tomorrow evening, about 6?"

I smiled. "Sounds great. There's an awesome little local coffee shop just down the road...."

"I know it," he said. "I'll meet you there."

Coffee is a fantastic drink. Especially, for me at least, when it's black and bold. I think the only valuable addition to coffee is the occasional shot of whiskey (and even that very rarely). Despite all the junk people put in it, coffee is a comforting, energizing drink. It's good for all sorts of occasions...including conversations.

Tim sat across from me at a tall, small round table on a warm Saturday evening out behind the small coffee shop, cradling a mug of steaming black coffee. Despite his truly massive and muscled frame, he was now wearing khaki cargo shorts, a t-shirt, and sandals. Seriously.

I looked like a scrawny, lanky dishrag next to him.

He blew on his coffee, took a sip, and looked up at me with a jovial countenance. "So," he said. "What was it you wanted to talk about?"

I looked back at him for a moment, then sighed. "I guess I'm just looking for some perspective."

"You want to know what I meant by my comment about the Norse pantheon yesterday," he said. It wasn't a question, so I just nodded in the affirmative. "I didn't mean to give any offense," he said.

"No, not at all," I said. "You didn't offend me. I've just...I've had similar thoughts, but I'm not sure what to make of them." I paused, uncertain, and looked up. "I mean...they're gods, and..."

Tim laughed, and not a little chuckle; it was a great, hearty belly laugh. He looked genuinely amused, and it confused me. "Says who?" he asked.

Well, that threw me for a loop. "What?" I asked.

Tim panted a little, then repeated, "Says who?"

"Well, all the old songs and epics...."

Tim burst out in another fit of laughter. Maybe my voice was breaking in an adolescent way, or I had something on my face or shirt? I inspected myself as inconspicuously as I could, and even looked over my shoulder, just in case. Tim held up a hand, and slowly forced himself to stop laughing. "Sorry," he gasped. "That never gets old."

I still sat confused, and I'm sure my face was plastered with a banner that just screamed "BAFFLED!"

"I...I don't understand," I said. "What's so funny?"

Tim continued looking at me with that big grin for a few moments, then composed himself further. "Okay," he said. "You're an intelligent guy. You've been studying the Old Norse for a while. Tell me: why are those old songs and epics written down?"

I considered that for a moment. "So that we would remember them and could pass them down," I said.

Tim shook his head slowly. "That's not our way," he said. "Think. It's right in front of you."

Insight flashed through my mind. "You're right," I said. "We're an oral tradition. Songs and epics, along with notable lineages, were painstakingly memorized by bards and sages, and passed down through recitation. Nothing of that sort was ever written down."

Tim nodded. "Keep going," he said. "You're almost there."

"*Who* wrote them down?"

Tim pointed a finger at me across the table, his lips compressed into a thin line. "That," he said, "is the right question." He thought for a moment, then added, "Consider the source."

"Says who?" I repeated Tim's question out loud. My mind staggered at how obvious it all was, and I struggled to fit the pieces together. "You're saying the Old Norse didn't see them as gods?"

"You know the old songs and epics," said Tim. "Where does the creation story start? You've already said it yourself."

"The creation story starts with Muspellheim and Niflheim and Ginnungagap," I said. "Fire and ice coming together in the void. A cow, Audhumla, licking the ice to feed herself and revealing the first...the first...oh!" I got it. "It's a lineage! The whole thing is a *lineage*!" I was astounded.

Tim nodded. "The Norse were a proud and brave people," he said. "Like all people, they asked the question 'Where do we come from?' Life in the northern reaches was hard and lonely. The only thing to keep them going in that cold, hard environment was inspiration. They knew they could get by because grandpa had."

"The Nordic path is all about ancestry," I said. I already knew this, but....

"Tell me," Tim said, "your favorite story about your grandpa. A time when you really needed him, and he was there."

The distraction was a welcome one, and I dove right in. "When I was a little kid, my Grandpa took me to his farm. He had some cows, and he let me help him feed them. We went down to the creek that runs through the farm, and while he cut some brush, I went fishing. I accidentally stirred up a big water moccasin, and it came up the bank toward me. I ran as fast as my little legs would take me back to the truck and climbed up into the bed, screaming the whole way. Before the six-foot-long snake reached the truck, Grandpa came out of nowhere, dived at the snake, grabbed its tail, came up in a military-style combat roll, wrapped it around a tree, and ripped it in half."

"Wow," Tim said. "That's amazing. How old was he?"

I thought for a moment. "Sixty-something, maybe?"

Tim was grinning again. "So...a sixty-some-thing-year-old man who's been out of the military for 40 years did a perfect diving combat roll at a sprint, and managed to grab a large snake's tail and wrap it around a tree without getting bitten, without breaking anything?"

I started to object, but Tim's gentle chuckle and raised hand stopped me. "I mean no offense," he said. "I'm just making a point. Are you scared of snakes?"

"Yes," I replied. "Terrified."

"So, your Grandpa saved you from one of your biggest fears in spectacular fashion. I could ask what really happened, but I doubt you'd remember." He paused for moment, then asked, "Do you see my point?"

I did. "Yes," I said. "You're saying that the songs and epics are somewhat exaggerated."

"No," he said. "Not exactly. Yes, it's probably true that the songs and epics have exaggerations in them." His brows knit together in thought. "Actually, it's extremely likely, given that the bards and sages who related them were probably singing for their supper, and a better story makes for a better chance at a meal. But more than that, my point is that these stories are intentionally *useful*. Like fairy tales, they provide a moral or situational guidepost."

I thought about that, sipping coffee.

"A lot like the story you just told me," said Tim.

It was time for my own eyebrows to get into the furrowing game. "I don't understand," I said.

Tim looked at me steadily as he sipped his own coffee. "Well," he said, "we've already jumped face-first down the rabbit hole, so tell me this: what's the point of religion?"

That was a seriously heavy question. I mean, come on. How do you answer a question like that? I decided to start simple and shallow. "To let people know who the 'real' god is, how to get to heaven, and how to avoid going to hell?"

Tim answered with another incredulous bout of laughter. "You don't mince words much, do you?" he said. I shook my head, smiling a little. "Well," he continued, "no. That's not the point."

"It's not?" I asked.

"No," he replied. "It's not." He paused, looking down at the table. "Are you familiar with the Bible?"

I nodded. "Some," I said. "I'm not an expert."

"You should read it," he said softly. "You've obviously read a bunch of religious texts. They all have something in common...apart from the three things you mentioned." He looked up from the table and said, "They're all pretty specific about lineage."

My eyebrows untangled themselves and raised. "Really?"

Tim nodded and said, "Really. The first few books of the Bible are chock full of lineage. Almost nothing else. My point is that religion is all about connecting to the Divine. For human beings, that has always boiled down to family lineage. It's much easier to connect to the Divine if Grandpa – or great-great-great-Grandpa – met Him."

"Oh," I said. Then the new info sank in a little deeper, and the puzzle pieces started thunking into place. "Oooooh," I continued, really starting to get it. "In the Bible, the creation story starts when God brings light into the darkness and creates the world out of the void. Then He creates Adam and Eve...the first humans...from whom all other humans derive." I stopped and looked up at Tim.

Tim was looking down at his cooling coffee. "Do you remember the names of the first humans in the Old Norse stories?" he asked.

"Askr," I replied, "...and Embla."

"Ash," Tim said, "...and Elm." He paused a moment. "Adam and Eve. Seems like a pretty big coincidence."

"Yeah," I said. "Coincidence. Sure."

Tim glanced up at me and said, "Take your time, brother. This is a lot to take in; a big pill to swallow. Don't choke on it."

I spent a while just breathing. I don't know how long, or when I stopped breathing. I had to close my eyes, to block out my surroundings. After several long minutes, I put my finger on the real problem that was giving me trouble. I had no context for this information. Just a monumental coincidence. Did one religion copy the other? There was no indication the two cultures were even aware of each other, until long after the events of the Bible were done. Centuries, in fact. So...what was I missing? I gritted my teeth, trying to complete the puzzle, sweating. I felt a broad, warm hand on my arm, and gasped, my eyes snapping open.

Tim was leaning across the table, his hand on my arm. His eyes caught mine and he said, "You need to relax. You don't have to know all the answers. Nobody does. Nobody."

I took a deep breath, nodded, and slumped forward to rest my head in my hands. Tim removed his hand from my arm, giving me some space to get myself back under control. After another couple of minutes, my breathing stabilized, and my posture relaxed. I sat back, taking a napkin from the holder on the table, and wiped the sweat from my face and neck. "Wow," was all I could say.

"Wow," Tim echoed. "Sorry for how that..."

"No," I said, cutting him off. "No apologies necessary. That's an important connection, and I needed to hear it. Thank you for that."

He nodded, once.

"I think I see your point," I continued. "We don't worship Adam and Eve as gods, and we're told not to worship Jesus, even though he was the Son of God. So why do we worship Odin, Thor, and all the rest?"

"You got it," Tim said. "They were..."

"...our ancestors," I finished. Tim nodded again.

"Thus the big question," Tim said. "Who wrote it all down?"

"Wait," I said. "You're saying that whoever wrote down all the songs and epics added the labels. They made Odin, Thor, Freyja, etcetera into gods and goddesses...but if the Old Norse people saw them as ancestors instead, then why make them into something bigger? I mean, if you're trying to discredit them, that seems a little counterintuitive."

"You're looking at it wrong," Tim said. I waited for an explanation while he swirled the dregs of his coffee. "Think controlled opposition."

"Controlled opposition?"

"Do you know what 'Satan' means?" Tim asked.

There it was. We were right back to me being a devil worshiper. I scoffed and drank some more coffee. I lit up a fresh cigarette, and sat back to level a narrow glare at Tim. "If I'm a devil worshiper," I said, "you are, too." I gestured at the hammer hanging around his neck.

He just stared at me for a moment, apparently dumbfounded. "Who called you a devil worshiper?" he asked. "I asked if you know the meaning of a word."

I cocked my head to one side, blowing smoke, and rolled my wrist to present an open palm to Tim, inviting him to explain.

Tim said, "Satan isn't a name. It's a sort of title."

"Huh?" It was all I could muster. Don't judge me.

"It's a Hebrew word meaning 'accuser,'" he replied.

"Accuser...as in 'enemy?'" I asked.

Tim shook his head slowly. "Not 'enemy' as much as 'opponent,'" he answered. "Think 'prosecutor.'"

I considered that, but the hamster in my head had apparently suffered a heart attack or gotten his wheel stuck or something. I just couldn't process it, so I shook my head.

Tim took the hint and said, "It's okay, brother. It takes some time to work through." He stood up, threw down a few dollar bills on the table, and offered me his hand. "I need to get home," he said. "Call me sometime, and we can talk again."

I stood up and shook his hand. "Thank you," I said.

He smiled and clapped me on the shoulder. "Any time," he said. Then he left, and I soon went home as well.

# Chapter Eleven

I knew from my own reading before I met this group of guys that there was a lot of misconception surrounding the Old Norse people. I mean, seriously: how could *an entire society* of people be nothing but brutal, bloody, mud-covered fuckers that rowed boats and raped people for a living? Two people who love each other and live together can't even agree on what to have for dinner most times. So, the concept of a whole set of nations constantly agreeing on that kind of lifestyle for hundreds of years at a stretch just didn't make sense.

The people I had come to trust gave me fresh perspectives that made more sense. Some of them were farmers. Some were hunters and gatherers. They lived in small tribes, but eventually crowned kings. They came together and conquered a large part of the world, and explored all over the globe when everybody else still thought it was flat. They were hard, proud people. So proud that they were fearless in spreading their culture and religion across the face of the globe. So hard and fearless that they gave the world a mindset that would allow the world to face insurmountable odds and always come out on top, or be happy to die trying.

So awesome that they were superior to everybody else. Wait, what?

I know, I know – it seems ridiculous when you say it out loud by itself. But when you're in between a rock and hard place, really struggling, and looking for a source of inner strength that will let you survive past the next meal, "because I'm white" seems almost logical. I came from a tough, proud, awesome line of people. That's got to mean something, right?

It was introduced to me little by little over the next several months. It's not like these people just came out during our first meeting and said "surprise, we're Nazis!" They're a closed, insular sub-culture that makes sure they can trust you before they drop a bombshell like that. They slip in a little here, a little there, and make it relate to what you're going through in life, as a justification for your hardships or a reason to blame somebody else. Their recruitment process is pretty brilliant. They take advantage of your situation as a means of convincing you.

When I saw the first swastika around the place where we all hung out, it was on one of those old World War II posters. I don't think I was meant to see it, but

I stumbled upon the poster and asked about it. I was told that he collected old war stuff, which wasn't a lie – he was always looking for one antique or another. I was also told the swastika was a rune, and that wasn't a lie either. That symbol has been around since forever, and is used – even today – by many cultures as a positive symbol of energy radiating in or out (depending on which way the forks are facing). So, step one – you come from a long line of awesome white people that have had to be hard and brutal because they had to deal with hard circumstances – just like you. Step two – there's nothing wrong with the swastika. Step three – Hitler did some crazy shit, but Germany was in a big fix and he was great for pulling the country out of the depths and getting the people rallied around a common cause that began the healing. You know where the term "Nazi" came from? It's short for the name of the political party Hitler founded: the NSDAP, or *Nazionalsozialistische Deutsche Arbeiterpartei*...which literally translates as "National Socialist German Worker's Party." Considering the times, that really wasn't a bad concept – a political party organized around the concept that Germans must work their way free of the political and economic oppression they faced. And considering my situation, a lot of hard work seemed like the only remedy to my problem.

Yes, the Nazis did horrible shit, and we all know it – the Holocaust was the worst of it. However, you'd be quite foolish to think the Nazis were the only ones to participate in that obscure branch of science called *eugenics*. Look it up. America did it too. We just weren't as obvious or prolific about it.

This could be a long and bitter story, but I'll keep it short as a way of showing my disdain.

To be honest, they never fooled me. Not really. Sure, a lot of the things they said were very convincing, and fit very neatly with my situation and my bruised feelings at the time, but I was never one to follow others down a path I knew was doomed just to fit in. Hey: I didn't fit in anywhere anyway. I was used to the feeling. So, I hung around and hoped my non-belief wouldn't be discovered – they're not very nice once you know about them and don't agree. Again, I need to be fair here – this was pretty much one guy, the leader of the group. Most of the others, I would later learn, were along for the ride just like I was. We were young, and angry, and lost, and we learned about the bullshit too late to bail easily.

I knew it would implode sooner or later, so I kept my eyes peeled for an opportunity to get out clean. In small, extreme groups, somebody eventually gets scared, and somebody else – usually leadership – gets paranoid. It's a volatile mix, and it only ends one of three ways: everybody gets busted, everybody dies, or everybody walks away.

The night it all went to hell, it was the most ridiculous excuse you could imagine for dissolving something that had been portrayed as so grand and glorious: an argument over a drunk girl. The leader (whose girl it was) decided he'd had enough and threw us all out – no exceptions. No fanfare, no fists or bullets flying, no flashing lights – just "everybody get the fuck out and don't come back."

I hopped in my car and blazed out just as fast as I could without raising any red flags that would throw suspicion on me.

"Have a care who you follow." Well played, good raven: the first of many tests, indeed. Simple words, for such a poignant warning. My first trial was complete, and I had learned a number of valuable lessons during that time. Patience and stillness in the face of pretty long odds was one. Another was self-reliance, self-worth, and confidence: if I was in a hard spot, I could absolutely get myself out of it.

Possibly the most important lesson I got from that trial? Extremists are true cowards who can't deal with the uncertainties that come of not having all the answers. They *have to be* right. It takes a strong, confident person to believe firmly in something and still admit that you might be wrong. It's hard to be open to new ideas about religion, or politics, or human rights – the big questions where nobody can ever really prove right or wrong, one way or another. It's much easier, much simpler, to walk in the Darkness. It's safer to only see in two shades, black and white. Him or me. With us or against us.

And that's all extremism of any kind is: *fear*.

No wonder my parents had such a problem with my spiritual seeking – they were *afraid* for my soul. Man, what an ass I'd been to think I could take a hard stand on something I didn't fully understand myself.

A month later – after nearly two years of homelessness and hard work and pulling myself out of the mess I'd made – I made the journey back to my parents' house. My mom met me at the driveway and cried in my arms for what seemed like forever. We talked for most of the day and night. The rest of the family joined in and welcomed me back as they came home from school or work. It was tough, and emotional, but rewarding in ways I can't describe.

The whole experience made me lose my faith a little bit. Look how much needless pain had come out of that ordeal. I still wanted to find my ancestors, to find that missing part of myself, but I had followed the wrong person, walked the wrong path – whether I participated in that last bit or not – and it had cost me more than I could bear.

After a long holiday weekend at home, I went back to my apartment and my job at the newspaper. I had given an oath not to give up no matter how hard it was, and my time for fear and mourning my mistakes was past. Time to find a new road, and forge ahead.

# Chapter Twelve

I stepped out of my apartment later that night to have a cigarette and got quite a shock. I lived on the second floor, and when I stepped out onto the balcony, I was confronted by a large raven sitting on the handrail directly outside my door.

I froze when I saw him, just staring.

He just stared back.

"Welcome, good raven," I said softly.

"How do you know that I am good?" he replied.

I just stared, my jaw dropping.

He began to cackle and hop from foot to foot. Snarky bird. "I joke," he said.

I shook my head and said, "Hell of a joke. Would you like to come in? I haven't seen you in a while."

"A while?" the raven asked. "You have not yet seen me, in this life."

*That* got my attention. "You're not the same raven I've been speaking with?"

"I am his brother," said the raven.

"His broth...."

"You could not tell us apart?" he asked, cutting me off. "Why? Because we all look alike?"

I didn't know what to say. "Well...you're both...."

"Black?" The raven cocked his head to one side.

"I was going to say 'ravens,'" I responded, lamely. "I don't know enough about ravens to...."

"Racist," said the raven. His beak was open, and I swear I saw his beady little black eyes shining with laughter. Was this feathery little prick baiting me?

"Relax," said the raven. "I am simply joking with you."

"Not funny," I said. "Especially given recent events."

"I think it's hilarious," sulked the raven, scratching the wooden rail he sat upon with the talons of one foot.

I sighed. "Well," I said, "it's not every day a talking raven shows up at my door. I presume you have a message for me."

"You presume...," said the raven, "...correctly." The raven spread his wings and ruffled his feathers, giving him a larger and more foreboding appearance. "A message I have for you, to restore your memory."

"In that case," I replied with a small bow, "be welcome to my hall." I opened my door.

The raven flew past me, into my apartment. I followed him inside and shut the door. So much for having a smoke.

That snarky raven was perched on the foot of my bed.

I sat down on my bed and said, "Okay. What's the message?"

"What? No food or drink or polite conversation?"

I sighed as the raven chuckled and did his little happy dance.

"I would apologize for my jokes," said the raven after a moment, "but that would be disingenuous of me."

I stared at him. "The message?"

"It's more of a tale," said the raven. "A long one. It's best communicated through a dream."

"You brought me a dream?" I asked. "Now you're the Sandman?"

The raven puffed his feathers and spread his wings again. "I am memory," he said, his voice considerably more ominous than before. I leaned away from him. "I am a guide through knowledge and experience. I am the living repository of all memory, the mirror upon which all reflect, and the path upon which all tread when seeking." After another moment of stunned silence, he settled down and refolded his wings. "My attempts at levity were for your sake," he grated softly. "I am far more than just a talking bird, and what I offer can be...heavy."

"My deepest apologies," I said, and meant it.

"Not necessary," he replied. "Many are disrespectful when first we meet. I am not beyond blame myself. You are not my first mortal charge, nor will you be my last." He was quiet for a few moments. "It is just that the harbinger-of-doom introduction gets old after a few millennia."

I wanted to laugh but glanced at the raven first. His eyes were twinkling again, so I gave in and chuckled nervously.

"Ready to begin?" asked the raven.

I nodded.

"Lie down and get comfortable," he said. "This will take the remainder of the night."

I lay down on the bed and wiggled around a little until I was comfortable.

"When you close your eyes," said the raven, "focus on...the beginning. Your beginning."

I did as the raven told me, focusing on my beginning as I closed my eyes. I immediately felt myself drifting off to sleep, and resisted for a moment, not sure I was meant to sleep. I gave in. I felt sure that if I was meant to be awake, the raven would peck me or something.

Time to trust the raven and walk my path from the beginning.

I was in darkness, until I opened my eyes. I'm not sure what I expected to happen, but it certainly wasn't this.

I opened my eyes and was assaulted by bright light. Not the light at the end of the proverbial tunnel, mind you, just really bright sunlight. I raised my arm to shield my eyes, and realized I was lying on my back on the ground. I blinked to clear my eyes and heard someone speaking to me. He wasn't speaking English, which freaked me out for a moment. "Huh?" I asked, squinting around my hand to get a look at the speaker.

The speaker was a young man, maybe early twenties, standing above me with his hand offered out to help me up. "Are your ears still ringing?" he laughed out. "I did not intend to hit you *that* hard," he said.

I took his hand and balked a little as I was hauled to my feet, because I was...squeaking and clinking. I looked down at myself as I came vertical and saw armor. Not a full set, and not plate armor. Mine was a well-worn and piecemeal set of leather and chainmail. On top of that, I was still looking up at the man who had helped me to my feet. Like, way up. I looked down again and shook out my limbs. Well, shit. I was a teenager. Maybe younger.

"Ready for another bout?" the man asked.

I looked down at the heavy sword blank and round shield on the ground, and shook my head. "Enough for today," I said. "I need to sit down, have a drink, and think this through." I stooped and picked up the sword blank and shield, and placed them in a waiting rack.

"Enough for today," the man echoed, nodding. He handed me a skin bag full of water, from which I drank. "Perhaps you should walk through the forest awhile," he continued. I looked up at him. "Maybe even a couple of days of solitude. I know a good spot down by the stream where it is quiet."

His suggestion sounded good, so I asked him for directions to this spot. Then I removed my training armor, picked up my regular gear – which included a short knife, a hand axe, a bow and quiver of arrows – and strapped it on. It was still early in the day, so I started walking.

The camping spot turned out to be better than expected. It was quiet, alright, aside from the basic
nature sounds: the gentle rustle of trees and grasses, the chirping of birds, and the ever-present bab-
bling and gurgling of the stream. The stream was
shallow and only about ten feet across at its widest
point. It was bordered closely on both banks by tall,
thick trees, except for the spot that was described
to me, which was clear of trees and underbrush. It
seemed...peaceful.

I stepped into the clear area. It was quiet, and peaceful, but...wrong. I closed my eyes and focused my
senses. I could hear something very, very faint that
almost sounded like singing. After just a moment it
faded away, and I decided I had better get started
making my camp. I dug a shallow hole and gathered
some large stones from the stream to make a fire
pit, then built a small fire in it. I set up a simple
lean-to shelter to sleep under. Then I cut down a
small sapling, carved it into a simple spear, and went
fishing.

Yes, fishing. I had started my day by getting my
bell rung multiple times, continued by hiking several miles through mountainous forested terrain,
and finished by building a temporary camp from
scratch. I was hungry. You try doing all that stuff in

a day at about 12 years old and see if you don't settle for a fish sammich.

Well, crap...I had no bread. Or seasonings. So, just plain fish fillets, then.

I caught two fish. Soon enough, the fillets were finished roasting over the small fire, and I was eating. From my seat by the fireside, I heard the flapping of large wings. I didn't startle, since I was expecting him. I laid the last of the fish fillets on a flat rock I had lain out earlier, then looked up at the raven. "Be welcome to my fire, Munnin," I said. "Please accept some food and rest your weary wings."

The raven ducked his head in a shallow bow, then ate a little of the fish. He looked up at me a moment later, puffed his feathers a bit, and said, "Now I understand why my brother likes you."

I chuckled a little and asked, "The food?"

"The food," he agreed. "It is good." He ate some more, as I laughed.

When he had finished eating, he hopped to the spring and drank. Then he hopped back and settled himself across the fire from me. "You heard the singing?" he asked me.

My eyes snapped up to his. "It was singing, then," I said.

The raven nodded, but didn't elaborate.

"I thought I heard very faint singing earlier, when I arrived here," I said. "But there was no source of it that I could see. It faded quickly."

"You did not follow it," the raven said.

"No, I did not," I said. I had to ask. "Who was singing?"

"The Fae," replied the raven quietly.

I felt my jaw just drop. It took me a few moments to recover enough to speak. I stared across the fire at the raven. "They are...they are real?"

"Very," replied the raven. "Their home is also your next stop on this journey."

I was stunned. I mean, how often do you hear that faeries are real, and you're on your way to visit them? My reaction? Redirection.

"Wait a second," I said. "You told me to focus on my beginning." I looked down at my pre-teen self, then back up at the raven. "This is it?"

The raven shook his head in agitation. "You are thinking too literally. Time is not linear. Did you think you were going to relive your birth? Which one?"

I stared, dumbfounded. "Which one?"

"You know the funniest thing about humans?" the raven asked. "You pride yourself on logic, but you don't use it. You believe in reincarnation, but think you were born only once, or that there must be a *first* birth, out of the hundreds, at some point in linear time. You are wrong, in the most fundamental of ways, but you do not see it." He stared hard at me for a long moment, then said, "Stop thinking like a limited, stunted human being. You want to be more than that, so *be more*."

That shut me up.

The raven gave a rasping sigh and said, "You asked me to show you this path, so walk it. Follow the singing." Then he took off and flapped his way into the distance.

I sat in the darkness for a while, staring at the fire until its flames had died out. Then I stared at the stars. I fell asleep after a bit…and that's when I heard it. The singing was back, a little louder than it was earlier. Perhaps it was only "louder" because everything else was quieter. In any case, the ethereal sound floated to me out of the darkness and stirred me awake.

I got up, strapped on my gear as quickly and quietly as I could, and tried to orient myself on the source of the music. I began walking toward where I thought it was coming from, narrowing my path as I went.

Deep in the forest I thought I saw a light, almost like a tiny fire. I strode toward it, and the singing got louder as I got closer.

I got close, really close, and realized that the light I saw was coming through some sort of...tear. I'm not sure how else to describe it. It was almost like the forest I was looking at were a painting, and someone had torn a small hole in it. The light and singing were coming through that small hole. I leaned down and put my eye to the hole, trying to see. Could it really be the Fae?

A shockingly beautiful green eye suddenly stared back at me.

I fell flat on my ass in the dirt.

# Chapter Thirteen

W hen the veil parted, I thought I was going crazy. The small hole began to expand vertically, like somebody pulling back a curtain to reveal a totally different place. It was a beach somewhere, the ocean waves rolling into the shore beyond what I could now see was a sizable bonfire. Figures stood all around the fire, looking at me. The singing had stopped. All was silent. A beautiful tall slender woman with shocking red hair and green eyes stood at the edge of the veil, holding it open with one hand. She beckoned me with her other hand, a gentle smile parting her lips.

I gathered myself to my feet, unsure of what to do. I wanted to accept the invitation, but I was also terrified. Were these the Fae?

The woman beckoned me again, still smiling.

"I am lost," I said. "I did not mean to intrude."

She nodded to me, and I heard her speak to me...but I heard her voice inside my head, not in my ears. *You did not intrude, young one. This is an invitation for you to join us, and we are most glad you have accepted. Come, and we will welcome you.*

I stepped slowly toward her, still unsure of myself. I could smell the salty air coming off the ocean, an occasional whiff of the harsh smoke. I could hear the gentle thunder of the waves breaking against the sandy shoreline, the sharp crackle of the bonfire's flames. It just didn't seem...real.

I looked directly at the woman again and heard her speak to me. *You have nothing to fear from any of us, child. This is not your first time to visit us. We know that you are seeking, and we offer only what is already yours. Your own memories.*

I swallowed hard and stepped through the parted veil onto the sandy surface of the beach. Behind me I heard a soft shifting sound, like soft cloth rustling. I turned my head to look for the source of the sound and saw...nothing but more beach and a stout tree line. My world, the forest I had just been walking through, was gone. My heart sped up even more, the fear palpable, as I looked back to the woman that now stood beside me. "I...I cannot..." I began to ask her.

"Go back?" she finished, and shook her head, still smiling. "No, young one. You did not return to your home the last time and have no need to return this time." At my blank expression, she smiled a little more widely. "Relax, dear boy," she said. "You have nothing to fear from us. You are seeking your past, and we play a small part in that story. We are simply a short stop on your journey."

I relaxed, just a little. I believed her. Still, I had just stepped foot into the realm of the Fae, and nobody does that without some apprehension unless they have less than two functioning brain cells.

I was pretty sure I had at least three. Hence, my reaction.

I drew myself up to my full height, facing the assembled Fae that were still staring at me. "Greetings and salutations, Lords and Ladies of the Sidhe," I said. "My name is..."

"Your own," said the woman beside me, cutting me off. Oh, right. Not wise to give them my name from my own lips. "We call you a name from our own tongue that you have earned: Aldoin." She smiled again and inclined her head to me in a gentle and courtly bow. "Welcome, Aldoin...to Alfheim."

*Alfheim*....

I bowed my head and closed my eyes....

...and opened them onto a simple wooden floor.

Startled, I glanced around. I was in a small wooden cabin. Judging by my appearance, I was also considerably older; an adult now, in my early twenties. What the...?

A soft blue light buzzed past a window quickly and gained my attention. I stared at the open window, with a candle standing lit on its sill. For a moment all was still and quiet. Then I could hear the buzzing noise returning, and suddenly the blue light flashed past the window again, and the candle went out.

I had other candles lit around the cabin, and a fire lit in the hearth, so one candle going out wasn't a big deal. Still, I had to know what had put it out. I walked as stealthily as I could across the cabin to the window, kneeling down so my eyes were just above the sill. I wanted to see what that blue light was about.

A tiny feminine figure leaped at my face from the side of the window and squeaked, "Boo!"

I fell on my butt again. Then I sighed. This was getting old fast.

"Oops!" squeaked the tiny figure. She put her hands over her face and began squeaking more. Was she laughing at me? I glowered. She continued laughing, her tiny face as red as a cherry. While she laughed, I tried to figure out what she was.

Sharp facial features. Long, straight, fine hair flowed over her head, neck and shoulders in a rich and shiny black waterfall. Light but strong wings sprouted from between her shoulder blades. She wore soft and almost shiny cloth of silver. She practically bounced with a jittery little flash of soft blue light every time she squeaked with giggles. She was also about three inches tall, not counting the wings.

A pixie, then.

I cleared my throat, a little noisily. The little pixie composed herself and gave a quick courtesy, then leaned a shoulder against the window frame, folding her arms and crossing her ankles. "Hello, Aldoin," she said.

"Hello...uh..." What was her name? I apparently knew her but couldn't recall her name. Well, crap. This should go swimmingly. This memory path thing needed some work, in my opinion. I decided to go with a small wave, a bright smile, and a dull, "Hi."

She raised a single, slender black eyebrow at my droll conversational skill, and stopped leaning against the window frame. Her arms remained crossed. Uh-oh. She *growled* – no kidding – and stomped a tiny foot, disturbing little dust motes into the air. "You," she said, "don't...remember...me!"

I tried to bluff my way out of it. I really did. I failed to come up with a convincing bluff, however, and settled for slouching down into a wooden chair with my face in my hands. "No, sorry," I said. "To be honest, I don't even remember how I got here."

"Oh!" she squeaked. She flew up in front of my face, then alighted on the edge of my small table beside me. "I understand! You are *seeking*!" She smiled at me and said, "You may call me...Rina."

I gave her a small bow of my head and smiled. "Hello, Rina."

She stood up, crossed her eyes, and waved lamely. "Hi," she said in a dull-witted voice. I laughed. I couldn't help it. She was doing quite an accurate impression of my foolish introduction. As I laughed, she giggled again. Then she plopped back down on the edge of the table and asked, "Okay, what are your questions?"

I stopped laughing and looked at her. "My questions?"

Rina sighed and began kicking her legs as they dangled off the table. "You cannot receive answers without asking questions," she said sagely.

"Okay," I said, "let's start at the beginning." I turned my chair to face Rina and asked, "What is seeking? What is happening to me?"

Rina looked up at me, cocking her head to one side. "You're not very good at this," she said.

"First time," I replied lamely.

She smiled and said, "No, it's not. That's okay, though, that you don't remember." She stopped kicking her legs, stood, and began pacing. "Seeking is like walking down a long, twisty path in a deep dark forest, looking for yourself." She stopped pacing and looked at me to see if I was following. Obviously, I wasn't. "What is a memory?" she asked.

"A memory is..." I thought out loud. "A memory is like a picture of something in the past."

"No," she said. She considered for a moment, a finger on her chin. "Well...not really. A memory is a captured moment of experience."

I had never thought of it that way, but it made a lot of sense. One thing nagged at me, but I couldn't quite put my finger on it.

"You think in terms of time," Rina cut in. "That a memory is something that happened before now."

"Yes?"

"You think of time as a straight line," she said. She chopped one hand into the other definitively as she explained. "I am born, I get big, and I die." She looked at me for confirmation. "Right?" she asked.

I nodded and said, "Yes."

"That is wrong," she said. She put her hands on her hips and looked at me as though that settled the matter.

"Huh?"

Rina's expression went from supremely confident to mildly disgusted and miffed. She puffed out a breath, blowing a stray strand of hair out of her eyes. "Where we are, right *now*, is a memory," she said. "Strictly speaking, this is an experience that you took part in more than two thousand years *ago*, according to your current notion of time, but it's not *then*...it's *now*."

I had to think this through for a moment, then began to get it. "Ahh...," I began. "You're saying that linear time is a kind of illusion. The reality is that all points in time exist at the same time." I looked a question at Rina.

She nodded, once. "The only moment...is *now*."

"I get it," I said, "but if that is true...what about the future? Why can't we see it?"

Rina considered a moment, doing something with her hands as though she were doing some hefty mental arithmetic. She nodded as she seemed to reach a conclusion, and said, "Some can, in a way. They have learned to play out circumstances in their own minds and see possibilities. It is a kind of experience, but because their knowledge is not perfect – and because of free will – it is not real-life experience, just a mental construct. So, it is always a bit flawed."

"We cannot see the future because we have not yet experienced it," I said.

"Yes," replied Rina.

I stood from the chair and paced around the table to the hearth. Above it was a shelf with several books upon it. "What are these?" I asked Rina.

She seemed to hesitate, which gave me pause. "That is your library," she said quietly. "Your collected memories."

I reached for a book, but before my hand could reach the shelf Rina darted in front of the books and spread her arms out. "No!" she cried out fervently, her face distended in an expression of fear and pain. I saw a single, silvery tear on one cheek, and pulled back my hand.

"What is wrong?" I asked her.

"Please understand," she responded, all but panting. "These are your memories, and I have no right to keep them from you, but…" She sagged a little. "Some of these memories are terrible enough to rip you asunder. I have a responsibility, as your guide, to help you choose your path." Her arms dropped to her sides and she choked out through little sobs, "Besides, it would wound me deeply to see a good friend destroyed by his own mind."

I took a single short step back and let my arms fall to my sides. "Very well," I said. "I trust your judgment, Rina. I accept you as my guide and will follow your lead." What she had just said troubled me. A lot. *Destroyed by my own mind?* That certainly didn't sound the least bit fun.

She let out a heave of a sigh, and quickly wiped the tears from her cheeks with a business-like nod. "Okay," she said. "Let me ask you a few questions, so I'm clear about exactly what you're seeking." She began to pace in front of the books, and I sat down again. After a few moments, she asked, "What do you want most?"

"Salvation," I said after thinking.

"Salvation..." Rina echoed slowly. "You want somebody to save you." She continued pacing for a moment, then stopped and looked at me. "From what?" she asked.

It was a perfectly simple and logical question, but it just stunned me.

"Uhh...I do not..." I took a few moments to think that through. I wanted to say "perdition," but that didn't make a lot of sense given the current context. My beliefs had changed over the past few years, and the Old Norse didn't really believe in...well, Hell. They had an icy analog, a frozen wasteland called Niflheim, where oath breakers were pursued and tormented by frost giants. They also had a fiery realm called Muspellheim, but I hadn't heard of anyone going there. Sure, they had a goddess named Hel, who presided over the "normal" dead, but her realm was more of a somewhat boring place where those who died of old age and natural causes went to chill and hang out and be a shade.

I wasn't an oath breaker, so why was I worried about going to the "bad" place?

My conversation with Tim briefly flashed through my mind, and it startled me. *Think controlled opposition*, his voice echoed in my mind. I drew in a sharp breath.

*I was still wandering.*

I turned my gaze back to Rina and said, "I'm not sure. I just feel that if I stay uninformed, if I continue to wander, my soul will be...lost." I'm not sure what made me use those words, specifically, but it felt right.

Rina's eyes brightened a few shades, and her lips turned up in a small smile. "Ahh," she said. "You are looking for the *way*."

"The...way?" I'm sure the nonplussed look on my face was all the clue Rina needed.

"The *way*," Rina said again placing special emphasis on the second word. She paused, as if trying to figure out the best way to explain it to me. I couldn't blame her. At this point I was wearing out the word "huh." So, I waited patiently.

"Humans are funny about the thing they call 'religion,'" she began. "Which basically means they are funny about faith. You have a thousand different names for divinity, and a thousand different paths to travel towards it. You humans also muddy the waters with a thousand rules. It is so confusing. No wonder you need a guide." She stopped talking and glanced nervously at me. "I mean no offense," she said.

"No offense taken," I said, smiling. "That is precisely my problem."

She nodded at me once, then shook her head a little. "Your problem is much bigger than that."

My face fell. "What?"

"Well..." Rina said, her voice trailing off. "Let's put it this way: intelligence is both a blessing and a curse."

"You're saying I'm too smart for my own good."

"Basically, yes," Rina replied. Before I could respond, she held up a hand to stop me and said, "Salvation of the spiritual kind is the simplest thing. All you must do is ask for it and mean it. Depending on which path you follow, you also need to follow some rules."

She began pacing again. "Pretty much all the books say so, anyway," she said. "Your real problem is that you have trouble with faith. Especially since you're intelligent enough to know that people lie when it suits them to do so, or that they can be easily deceived when there is no proof. Hence, the concept of faith is troublesome for you." She turned to me and said quietly, "You don't want to just believe. You want to *know*."

I interjected, "The *way*. I am looking for the commonality shared by the religions."

"More accurately, you are seeking the truth about the Divine," Rina said.

"Yes," I replied.

"That is a very twisty path, Aldoin," Rina said. "You have chosen a very difficult path."

"True," I acknowledged. "For me, it is the only path worth treading."

Rina's eyes welled up with tears again. "It will be painful for you, and very dangerous," she said quietly.

I considered that but nodded. "I must know."

Rina bowed her head, fresh tears sliding down both cheeks. "It could destroy you...."

I reiterated, "I *must know*."

She heaved a big sigh and wiped her cheeks again. "Very well," she said. "Promise me something?"

I nodded and replied, "If I can."

"Always," she said, "no matter what you learn during this seeking, remember that you have friends and family *now* that love you, and that it is worth continuing."

That was a little shocking but matched up with a promise I had made to the first raven. "No matter the cost," I said, "I stand fast."

Rina nodded reluctantly and touched the spine of the first book on the mantle. "Okay," she said. "Let's go back to the beginning." The book floated to the table and opened to the first page as it settled gently upon the surface. I turned to face the book, and Rina alighted on the tabletop beside it.

"Please remember your promise, Aldoin," she said. "I know I am belaboring this point, but I must impress upon you just how dangerous this will be. A memory is a captured moment of *experience*. It is not knowledge, nor wisdom. It is *experience*. Memories are *living* moments. Down this path, you will be *re-living* some of the worst horrors you can imagine. Do not get stuck in these moments. Remember who you are *now*."

"I will," I said, trying to ignore the queasy feeling in my gut.

Rina nodded again and placed the fingers of her left hand on the first page of the book. She beckoned me closer with her other hand, so I leaned forward. She touched the tiny fingers of her right hand to my temple and said softly, "Remember." I closed my eyes, took a deep breath....

# Chapter Fourteen

... and opened them onto a scene I could hardly imagine.

"Papa!" cried a young girl's happy, shrill voice. Bubbling giggles and the patter of small feet came across the room at blurring speed, and I let out a hefty "Oof!" as the little girl leapt on top of my chest and threw her arms around my neck, burying her face in my neck.

I hugged her tight and asked, "Time to wake up, little one?"

"Yes, Papa," she said. "Mama is cooking breakfast, and she says she needs eggs." She looked at me with wide, beautiful, ice-blue eyes and asked, "May I go with you?"

I gave her a sidelong glance and said, "That depends on whether you can get ready for chores before me."

I glanced at my standard clothing hanging on pegs on the wall across the room. "Go!" I said and started to sit up. I gave another "Oof!" as the small girl leapt up and pattered across the room, giggles galore.

I watched her go. She was about five years old. My daughter....

Her mom was waiting for eggs. Better get started. I dressed rapidly.

I turned to the room's door as I began strapping on my sword belt and saw my daughter standing there, still wearing the simple sleeping shift, to which she had added sandals. She was holding a small basket, too, and bouncing on the balls of her feet with simple, undiluted excitement. *She loves those chickens*, I thought.

"Okay, let's go see if Mama needs anything else first, and then we'll go visit the chickens," I said. The little girl squealed and turned to run to the kitchen. I followed.

I arrived in the kitchen to find my wife busy at the hearth. The smell of fresh bread baking mingled with the scents of hot herbal tea and sausages roasting. My wife stood up from the hearth, a tall blonde, slender but stout. She looked around and spotted me and smiled. I gave her a warm hug and a kiss, and I could swear I was already standing in the afterlife. "Eggs will be enough before breakfast," she said. "After that I have a list. Those are our last sausages, so you'll need to hunt soon."

I smiled and said, "I know. I will set out after we eat." Then I turned to my eager little helper and said, "Let us go and get some fresh eggs, young one." She was already standing by the door.

We had a little coop for the chickens with a large, enclosed yard for them to wander and graze in. My daughter ran up into the coop and began gathering eggs. When she finished she handed me the small basket, and then went out into the enclosed yard with a sack of feed. I smiled and laughed as she pranced around like a chicken, sowing the mix of grains and nuts for them to peck at. She knelt down with some feed in one hand and petted a couple of the chickens that came to her. It was adorable.

After a few minutes of this I called her back to me and handed her the basket of eggs, which she carried back to the house. Her mother took the basket when we returned, and within minutes we sat down to enjoy a hearty breakfast.

After the simple but filling meal, I gathered my hunting things together, adding a bow, a quiver of arrows, and a spear to my sword and dagger. I would need to find a good boar and, if I could find one, a deer or (better yet) an elk. If I could kill one of each, we would be good for meat until winter set in, just over a month from now.

I took my gear out to my horse and made sure everything was ready to go. Now for the hard part: saying goodbye to my wife and daughter. My wife was well-versed in fencing and archery. I had seen to that myself not long after we were married. I always got a little nervous leaving her and the young one alone, though. Especially over the past year, as the raiding parties had gotten worse. We had not seen or heard of the raiders for the past couple of seasons, and the house was a veritable fortress now, since I had reinforced it over the summer. They would be okay for a day while I hunted for food. I had to have faith, in my wife's fighting ability if nothing else.

I turned away from the horse and found my wife and daughter standing there to bid me farewell. My wife handed me a small package of food and gave me a long, strong hug and a kiss. "Good hunting," she told me with a fierce smile.

"I will be back by tonight, I think," I said. "Noon tomorrow, at the latest." She nodded and stepped back from me.

The little one took the opportunity to rush me and hug my legs. "Don't go, Papa!" she cried out. She was crying, of all things. She had not done this before.

I knelt down and hugged her tight. "What is wrong?" I asked her.

She looked me in the eyes and said, "I had a bad dream."

"Well," I said, "I will be back soon as I can, and we can talk about your dream then. Okay?"

She shook her head vigorously and hugged me tight again, burying her face in my neck amid sobs. "I need to get us some food," I said. "When I get back, maybe you can sleep in our bed for a few nights until you feel better." I glanced up at my wife, who was frowning at the little one's unexpected distress. She nodded.

I peeled the little girl away from me and planted a gentle kiss on her forehead. "I will be back tonight," I said. "I need you to stay here with Mama and keep her safe...and the chickens."

She wiped her runny nose on a sleeve and nodded, mastering herself. "I love you, Papa," she said.

"I love you, too," I said. Then I stood, mounted the horse, and started for the tree line. I looked back and saw them standing in front of our home, waving at me. I waved back.

# Chapter Fifteen

I opened my eyes in my own bed, in the here and now, and sat up. I stretched and yawned, and looked at the foot of the bed, where the raven was apparently still sleeping with his head tucked under a wing. It wasn't "just a dream," then. Damn.

That last part, with who I remembered as my wife and little girl, bothered me in a very unsettling way. I had a bad feeling that memory wasn't complete. But then, why had I awoken?

"It is morning," said the raven, and I just about jumped out of my skin. I most definitely did not squawk like a small startled woodland creature. The raven cackled anyway and continued, "You have work soon. I suggest a good shower."

I gave the raven a brief sardonic glare, then realized he was right and shrugged. "I'll do that," I said. "Anything I can do for you first?"

"Two things," he said. "Open that window so I can leave, for starters." I walked to the bedroom window and opened it on the humid pre-dawn. He flapped over to the window sill and looked at me directly. "Remember your promise and know that despite what you learn about your past, you must still exist *now*," he said. "Do not forget that you have family and friends who love you and need you *now*." I nodded. "I will return tonight," he said, and then took wing out of the window and flew away. I closed the window and began to get ready for my day.

I returned to my apartment early that evening and prepared a hearty meal for myself. I had not eaten anything all day and had a feeling I'd need the sustenance for tonight. It didn't take long before I heard a sharp tapping on my bedroom window. I pushed back from the table and went to open it for the raven.

The raven stepped in through the open window and flapped his way to perch on the foot of the bed. "I made some food," I said. "You hungry?"

The raven gave me a shrewd look. "You are trying to bribe me," he said.

I threw back my head and let out a belly laugh. "Not hardly," I said. "Though it couldn't hurt, right?"

The raven's shrewd look didn't waver in the slightest. "I don't do pornographic dreams," he said.

I laughed again, harder this time. The raven cackled, too. I sat down on the bed and looked at him. "Can I ask you questions about what I see in these...memories?"

He looked at me directly and responded, "You cannot receive answers without asking questions." My eyebrows shot up as he quoted Rina, but before I could ask him anything he said, "Of course you may ask questions, but I – and all of your guides – are limited in how we may respond. Knowledge is not the same as experience, and it is almost always preferable that you experience the memories afresh to gain a better understanding."

I considered that. Another reference to the difference between knowledge and experience. It seemed that this was becoming a common thread. What were they trying to get across to me?

The raven broke into my reflection with an unexpected answer. "You have been stabbed."

"What?" I asked, then noted that he was pointing his beak at my right side, near my hip. "Oh, that."

I had been stabbed there about a year previous, during a sword fight. No kidding, I had been a member of a live-steel guild that fought with real weapons, generally only to "first blood." During the fight in question, I had already won – twice – and the guy I was fighting had already broken the rules once by conceding the match (called "yielding") and then continuing to fight when he thought me off guard. Classic dirty fighting with a cheap shot meant to surprise. The second time he was on the ground and had yielded, having dropped his sword and shield, he did surprise me, with a dagger to the inside of my hip as I went to help him up. I had dropped my sword when I was stabbed, it hurt so freaking bad, so when he picked up his sword and regained his feet, I dodged, took his sword, and took his right hamstring. Then I had to carefully and painfully remove the small dagger lodged near my pelvis. I learned several hard lessons that night.

"Yes," said the raven. "That is exactly the point. You talked to several others before that happened, a couple of whom had been stabbed themselves. You saw it happen uncounted times in films. Did any of that actually prepare you for the bite of sharpened steel into your flesh and bone?"

"No," I replied.

"So, you have your first answer," said the raven. "You may ask questions, but there is no substitute for personal experience. There is a vast difference between an academic understanding and experience. Me? I am watching a movie. You...you are *living* it."

"I understand," I said.

"I see that you do, now," said the raven. "May I offer you a piece of advice before we begin?" he asked me.

"Please," I said.

The raven ducked his head in a brief nod. "You have met your wife and daughter from many, many lifetimes past. You are correct in thinking that memory was not complete. There is much, much more to that memory." He paused for a moment, as though picking his words carefully. "The events of that time have colored all of your lifetimes since, even up to the present day, and are the primary reason for your current seeking."

"Family," I interjected, feeling a surge in my emotions that brought a sudden welling of tears to my eyes and stole my breath. I felt like the floor beneath my feet was shifting and a quick gut jerk that signaled I was about to fall.

"Do not think about them," the raven's words cut through my weak moment like a dousing of icy water, bringing me sharply back to my senses. I gasped and looked at him. "You have been a...well, to those you see as threats, you have been a walking doom...for *millennia*. You are very rarely wrong about such judgments, but you do get, uh, *over-en-thusiastic* about it at times. More importantly, this self-imposed role takes a serious toll on you, partic-ularly over the long term. It changes you, transforms you. Those brands are no accident, son."

I pulled my left sleeve up to my shoulder and glanced down at my outer bicep, where the Futhark runes for life and death had been burned into me with a wood burning iron and a cigar, a couple years previously. Now they were established scars. "They're not?" I asked.

"No," said the raven. "They were intentionally chosen for you, and placed just so, for very specific reasons."

"They were chosen and burned into me by a member of the group I was part of, which broke apart in a nasty way not too long ago, because he went kinda crazy," I said.

"A tool is a tool, and nothing more than that," the raven said. "It still needs a hand to guide it." He considered for a moment, then said, "You also have a brand on your rib cage, on the left side where it is close to your heart. Odal, which represents...."

"...Family," I finished.

He nodded again and met my eyes. "In light of what you have begun to realize about your past and present," he said, "do you really still believe it is an accident you pulled that particular rune out of the bag?"

"I guess not." He was right, of course. I had drawn that rune out of a full bag, seemingly at random, but there was just no chance it was random. Not given my situation at the time, and especially not given what I had learned since then.

"Listen to me," the raven said. I looked at him. "You will not see that woman and girl again for some time. You will be working backwards from now on, to get a better understanding of the greater context, before you experience that...horror. It will help you to not make the same choices going forward. At least, that is our hope. That your ire may be tempered."

"I've been that...bad?" I asked. I didn't think of myself as any kind of monster....

The raven shook his head vigorously and snarled, "Subjective terms again. You have actually done a great measure of good...but the toll it has taken on you is too great for our liking. You have spoken to soldiers who came back from wars from the past century. Your grandfathers are two of them. They are...*haunted*...by the horrors of their small parts in a single war. You are a good man – always have been – but try to imagine what a *hundred* wars would do to a man."

My throat constricted a little. "A...a hundred?"

"In your case, the number of battles is closer to a *thousand*."

I began to tremble.

"Let me add this little fact to the heap, so you may better understand the gravity of the situation we are trying to remedy with this seeking," said the raven. "You are aware of the Allfather's stoic nature?"

"Yes," I answered. "He is not one for showing emotion."

The raven nodded, ducking his head, then leaned in close enough to whisper in my ear. "He has *wept* for you."

I gasped and stood up, my whole body trembling now. I rushed to the bathroom and vomited, then splashed cold water on my face. When I returned to the bedroom, the raven was still perched on the footboard, right where he'd been when I left. He looked up at me as I entered the room and followed me with his gaze while I sat on the bed again. "You have many deep and painful scars, Aldoin. We cannot heal them or wipe them away, but we can help you understand them," he said. "Understanding is the way to the peace you seek."

That made an uncomfortable amount of sense, given my emotional state. "Okay," I said. "I will do my best to understand what I experience during this seeking."

The raven said softly, "No hard thought necessary, yet. Just live it. Understanding will come."

I nodded agreement and lay down on the bed, set-tling my head upon the pillow. "I will be ready in just a few moments," I said. "I need to breathe."

"You are learning already," said the raven.

"Don't get all excited," I told him, letting my eyes drift closed. "I'm still trying to decide whether or not I've gone insane."

The raven cackled, and my world went black.

# Chapter Sixteen

I opened my eyes to a campfire. It was very dark, either late night or very early morning.

Somebody shook my shoulder gently, and I turned my gaze up to find a familiar planes-and-angles face, framed with a red beard and long red hair. "Liam?" I asked.

He looked a question at me for a moment, then answered with, "Well, I'm not the damned jester."

I laughed. I couldn't help it. I took his offered hand and let him haul me up to a sitting position. "Sorry," I said. "Sleep sometimes throws me off."

He handed me a small bowl of wild game stew with a few biscuits on top and said, "We found them. Other side of the loch and a couple hours' walk through the forest." He put a wooden spoon into his own bowl of stew and began eating. "You been traveling the other side again?" he asked.

"Something like that," I answered noncommittally. I tried a biscuit drenched with the stew and gave a low groan of pleasure. "This stew is excellent, Liam. You may not be the jester, but you would make a damn fine cook."

He grunted through a mouthful, then said, "I had to do something. That ridiculous fish soup we had last night gave me the trots." He glared across the fire toward another man. "I have been shitting all night." The man across the fire hung his head, shaking it.

It was early morning, then.

Liam and I finished our stew in silence, then he turned to me. "What is our plan of attack?" he asked.

I couldn't remember the situation, because apparently playing sock puppet with my past self didn't always entitle me to my memories. "Refresh my memory," I said. While he spoke, I let my eyes drift closed and tried to at least remember where I was. The language we spoke was vaguely familiar, as was the surrounding landscape. It was cool, even though I knew it was the summer season. And we were referring to a body of water as a loch. Scotland, maybe?

I looked down at myself and saw buckskin breeches and boots and shirt. So, we were Picts.

"It started two days ago when the raiders hit our village," Liam said. "We don't know who they are, only that they are cowards. They hit us in the night and killed a lot of our people. Burned some of our homes, and..." His pause made me open my eyes and look at him. He was obviously distressed, and barely containing his rage. A tear rolled down one cheek.

An instinct within me made me reach out and grasp his shoulder. "We'll get him back," I said. I can't believe I didn't remember this when I woke up in this body. I'd have to speak to the raven about this. Liam's son, about ten years old, had been taken, along with several other young children.

Liam sniffed and gave a curt nod.

"We go in quietly, find the children, disable their means of escape, and then take them out," I said. "None of the raiders will walk away from this. Not one. You have my word." I glanced around the fire and noticed everyone listening to me.

Liam looked at me with a face carved from stone. "Thank you, brother," he said.

I stood, shaking my head, and said, "Thank me after. Right now, we have a job to do." I clapped my hands together once and looked around the fire at the dozen or so men. "Half of us on their back trail, the other half approaches them from the trail ahead. Start with bows and take out any lookouts. Find the children and remove them to safety, quietly. Disable any means of escape. After that, we round them all up and take our vengeance. Do we have knowledge of any boats on this side of the loch?"

A man on the other side of the fire said, "Yes. There are three small boats just up the shore. I spoke to their owners earlier, and they left them for us." He looked in the direction of the small village. "They were hit yesterday, same as us," he added.

"Good," I said. "Leave the horses hobbled here so we can make better speed and approach them by stealth. Take only water and weapons. Let's move."

They all moved quickly and with purpose. When we were ready to go, and the fire had been put out, I pointed to the man that had spoken earlier. "Take us to the boats."

When we landed on the opposite shore of the loch, I split us into two teams and said, "Until we have the children safely away, hand signals only. I want the best stealth approach we can make." They all nodded, and we set out.

I cannot describe the feeling of running through a forest in the dark. You must know the land, to avoid tripping and running headlong into trees and such. Even with the moonlight, which was bright, you must have an intimate knowledge of the terrain to remain sure of your footing and not break yourself, and to remain quiet. Liam had said the raiders were "a couple hours' walk" through the forest, but that included tracking them.

We made the trip in about fifteen minutes.

Our bows sang in near unity, and the raiders' watchmen dropped like marionettes with their strings cut. It wasn't silent but wouldn't be enough to rouse anyone from sleep. Nothing stirred in the camp. After a few moments of watching to make sure, I signaled and we all moved in except four that stayed concealed in the forest with their bows ready. They would cover our backs while we got the captive children out.

We found them quickly enough, in a makeshift cage of hewn timbers. Their hands were all bound, but their feet were free to move, which was good. It was relatively simple to open the cage, and to get the children moving. They were tired and hungry and scared and weak, but they were okay. I cannot describe the relief I felt at discovering that...or the red rage that boiled up inside me after.

Liam stepped up beside me and said softly, "The kids say they were the only captives. A few women were taken as well, but they were raped and killed the first day, because they resisted or tried to escape." He paused for a moment and then said, "My son is alright."

"I'm glad for that," I said.

Liam nodded and then said, "Time for vengeance?" I noticed he was holding a great battle axe, his favored weapon, clutched to his chest, his hands wringing the haft as though strangling it.

"Yes," I replied, and drew two short swords. I raised one over my head, gave a ringing shout, and chopped it down. Then the chaos of joined battle ensued.

There turned out to be around fifty raiders, against our dozen. The four archers I'd left in the tree line took down any runners and protected our backs. Not a single shaft missed its mark. A fierce pride roared through me as I danced through the enemy ranks, blades whirling. I caught a glimpse of Liam swinging the axe at an enemy and saw a mass of wet ruin spin away.

All told, it took twenty minutes to finish the fight, pile all the raiders in the makeshift cage – some of them not quite dead yet – and tear down their camp, piling the makings atop them. I found a small store of cooking fat and threw it around the base of the pile. I heard a makeshift torch take light and spun to look around. Liam was walking toward the stacked cage with the small fire in his hands. I stepped in front of him and held out my hands. "I will do it," I said.

Liam met my eyes and bristled. "My son..."

"Is safe and waiting for his father," I said, my voice hard. "You have taken your vengeance...but this will leave a stain." Groans of anguish and fear came from the cage, backing up my words. "You do not need this on your conscience, brother."

Liam stood fast for a few more moments, then seemed to deflate a little as he passed me the fire. "Thank you," he murmured.

"Go to your son, and keep his attention off this," I said. He nodded and turned away. I raised my voice to carry to the rest of the men. "That goes for all of you. Start taking the children back to the boats. I will catch up to you."

When they had all gone, I set fire to the cage. I watched as it caught and crackled and popped. I heard a few choking coughs, and a few agonized screams that trailed off into wails of despair. I watched until I was absolutely sure not one of them would live to repeat this kind of horror another day, and the roaring flames had dwindled.

Then I walked back to the boats.

We arrived in the village by the loch just after dawn and were greeted by grateful weeping mothers and stunned fathers, accepting their children back with a hungry and desperate embrace. They fed us all out of gratitude, along with handshakes and thanks.

It was a little more heartbreaking when we returned to our own village. Even one dead was too many, and we had suffered far more than one loss during the nighttime raid. I saw Liam reunited with his wife, who was hugging their son. I saw a little girl standing near them, crying quietly. Both her parents had been lost, and their home burned down. Liam went over to her and put an arm around her shoulders, guiding her back to his family. He was taking her in. He was a good man, and I was proud to know him.

I spent the remainder of the day cleaning and sharpening my blades, checking my bow and arrows and other gear, and tending to my horse and my own minor wounds. I watched the sun set, and the moon rise. I spent all this time alone, thinking to myself. I had no family to return to: no wife, no children, no siblings, a father dead in some senseless conflict, and a mother dead of age and illness. I had been alone like this for more than a decade. The only people I had for family were the people of the village, and I wouldn't intrude on their private lives no matter how welcome they made me feel.

When the stars had been out a while, I laid myself down on the soft grass and closed my eyes to sleep. They were safe, and already beginning the long and painful process of mourning and healing. I couldn't ask for more than that.

# Chapter Seventeen

W hen I woke up, I was in a teepee.

Yes, a teepee.

No, I'm not joking.

I really need to have a word with my supernatural, black-feathered travel agent. I sighed and sat up.

To be fair, it was astoundingly cool to be in this time-jumping, memory-living, real-life-in-a-dream-state position. I was learning loads about myself and history...but the transitions were jarring, disconcertingly so. He couldn't just tell me where I was going?

*Me? I am watching a movie. You...you are living it.* The raven's words answered my question well enough. My memories, my path, my seeking. I was probably guiding myself at this point, at least in some measure.

Appraising myself, I determined that I was a young brave. About 19, maybe? Thin but well-muscled. I saw a bow and quiver of arrows nearby, along with a stone tomahawk and a viciously sharp flint knife.

A young girl, about twelve, burst through the flap of the teepee. She was heaving breath, apparently disturbed about something. Sunlight came in with her. It was morning, but only just past dawn. I squinted my eyes against the sudden brightness and turned my face away. "Little sister? What is wrong?" I asked.

I heard the thunder of hooves and felt the ground tremble beneath me. "They are coming!" she screamed. Then, as suddenly as she had appeared, she was snatched away. I sprang to my feet, startled, and stared at the arch of the open teepee flap she had just occupied. *What is happening?*

As I stared, I heard a brief ripping noise behind me, and a flaming arrow whipped past me before burying itself in one of the wooden frame posts with an angry, quivering wasp whine. Screams and shouts and thundering hooves and the whipping whistle of arrows flying rent the air. *We are under attack!*

I scooped up my weapons and rushed out of the flap ready to fight. That was very nearly a fatal mistake. As I ran I felt a sharp sting in my left calf and tumbled to sprawl on the ground. An arrow stood in my lower leg, leaking red blood. I broke the feathers off the shaft and pulled it through, stifling a scream of agony. I crab-scuttled backward to my teepee, which was on fire now, and cut a long strap of hide from its wall to bind tightly around my bleeding leg. I took a moment to collect myself and wall away the pain, and to look around.

We had been caught unawares and were paying for it in blood...and children. As I watched, two more young ones were scooped up by men on horseback as they mourned over their fallen parents. Many of our teepees were on fire, and men and women were running, and fighting, and dying. They had taken my little sister, the only family I had left to me.

Enough. I would not stand for this. I would not abandon her to them.

*Great Spirit*, I prayed silently. *Father of my fathers and Creator of the Infinity, I call upon you for aid. I need to keep my strength for a while longer. Make my eyes sharp, my feet swift, and my heart strong. My sister and so many others have been taken from their homes, from their families by a Great Evil. Help me to bring them home and put an end to this scourge.*

I stood, the pain in my leg like a smoldering fire that both foretold my end and drove me forward. I gathered my weapons again and strode to my horse. The beautiful creature was made restless by the smells of fire and blood and the anguished wails of mothers. The other activity had subsided. The cowards had hit us, taken the children, and run.

They would not get far.

I mounted my horse, calming it with my hands on its head and neck and softly spoken words. It responded favorably, and when I was confident the animal was back under control, I signaled it forward with a gentle press of my heels. As I rode through my ravaged village, I spotted an old woman weeping over the body of a young man, presumably her son. She lifted her eyes to mine, and her face went slack for a moment, her weeping stopped. She raised an arm and pointed to indicate where the cowards had fled with the children. I nodded and turned my horse to follow the direction she indicated.

I could see the trampled tall grasses where their horses had torn it up in their hasty retreat. I followed the trail, first at a walk, then at a trot. After a short time, I crested a hill and could see them, still riding as fast as they could, whipping their horses into a lather. There were ten of them.

Two of the biggest advantages of really knowing your land: knowing the ways into and out of it and knowing where it ends. Just by their direction of travel I knew where they were going to have to cross out of my land, and how long it would take them to reach that place. I turned my horse off their trail, heading now for the narrowest and shallowest portion of the river. I could reach it first and ambush them by midday.

I reached the twenty-foot-wide shallow section of river within an hour of hard riding and found a spot along the bank to conceal my horse beneath an old willow tree. I had been here many times over the years, but this time something made me stop and stare at the tree. It was beautiful, in full bloom, and it tickled something in the back of my mind. I shook off the ominous feeling and got to work setting my trap.

My first priority was to stop their progress. If even one of them got away, we would have more trouble on our hands in short order. Second, I had to make their greater numbers count against them. Third, I needed a fighting position that would provide enough cover but not obstruct my own ability to shoot the bow. Fortunately, this spot had all three of those covered in abundance.

I started by breaking a few tree branches on the opposite bank of the river that were just tangled with vines. They used to hold those vines high above the only trail through the underbrush on that side of the river. Now, they hung in the vines across the trail as a potentially deadly obstacle to anyone on horseback. That mess would need to be cleared before anyone could reach the trail. Forward progress stopped.

Our side of the river was just as heavily wooded as the other side and had just as much underbrush. I went to the deeper portions of the river and cut enough thorny material to stretch across the river from bank to bank twice. Using stones in the river to secure some of the material in place, I lined both sides of the path across the river to about knee-height. No horse would willingly chance crossing it unless they could jump it...and if they were forced to jump into the deeper water, they would likely drown. These horses were tired, too: they were each carrying more than their one usual rider, and they had been driven into a lather already.

So, they could not run away unless they wanted to risk drowning their horses, and they would not risk running back through our territory after what they had done. That meant they would try to clear the obstacle across the trail and would stay in the seeming safety of the shallows until it was done. Of course, I would be on my side of the river.

The "kill box" was ready. I found a spot to hide in the underbrush and waited.

It did not take long.

When they came, they came in a rush, all bunched up. The fools had pushed their horses to the point of exhaustion, and the animals refused to either tangle with the mess of vines or jump in the deep water. They stopped and drank the shallow water rushing around their hooves. One actually dumped its rider – and the two little ones he had abducted – onto their backsides in the water.

I began. I could describe all the gory details, but instead I will limit myself to the salient points. Seven fell to my bow. Two fell by my tomahawk. One fell with a sharp twist of his head that broke his neck. Just to be sure none of them tried this again, I cut all of their throats.

I made sure all the children were alright, including my little sister, and had them help me collect the horses so we could all ride back to the village. When we arrived back at the village it was about how you would expect: weeping mothers, stunned and relieved fathers, and all the rest.

I fell off my horse. Apparently, I had worked the makeshift bandage on my leg loose at some point. I had bled out.

My sister appeared in my vision, crying. I pointed to our shaman and said, "He will care for you, and see to it that another family takes you in as their own." He nodded to me.

"No!" my sister cried. "Do not leave me!"

"You are home with our people, and safe," I said, my voice thready and weak. "I love you, little sister."

*Thank you, Great Spirit. Thank you...thank...you....*

# Chapter Eighteen

I opened my eyes and saw a fire in front of me. There were several other people sitting around the fire. They were all focused on a man that circled the fire telling a story. I recognized it as a Celtic tale about the Tuatha. I recognized the man, too: tall, slender, corded with lean muscle, with long red hair, pale skin, and large green eyes. His name was Gweilt. Cu Gweilt. He was a shaman, or what passed for one in the ancient Celtic society.

He was also a good friend of mine. I called him "brother." For all I knew in the moment, that could be a literal truth. He was wearing buckskin pants and moccasin boots, no shirt, and some kind of ceremonial mask. I could also see a silver torc around his neck, its ends carved in the likeness of wolves' heads.

I held a clay cup of some hot liquid and took a sip of it. It was tea, I think. Strong and heady in its aroma and taste. It was good, and somehow cooled me down, taking the edge off the heat of the fire and the balmy night.

I closed my eyes and listened to the tale. I'm not sure how long I sat like that – it could have been a few minutes, or a few hours – but when I opened my eyes, it was quiet except for the crackle of the fire, which had died down to small licking flames and embers. Hours, then.

I felt, more than saw, my brother Gweilt walk up behind me. "You wanted to speak to me, brother?" he asked. I knew that I hadn't asked him, but he always seemed to know when a person was seeking his counsel. I smiled and looked over my shoulder at him. I patted the large fallen log I was using for a seat. I pulled a small skin of liquor from the ground beside me and poured a little into the clay cup. I offered it to him as he sat, and he took it. With a small raise of the cup, a silent toast of sorts, he downed the contents.

"You are here for the drink," I jested, still smiling.

He shrugged and said, "You have the good stuff." He didn't miss a beat. It was hilarious. I laughed. He laughed with me. The levity felt good after my recent experiences of pain, and blood, and death. I hated to break the moment of respite, but I did need his counsel.

"My dreams have been dark of late, brother," I said.

Gweilt let his head nod forward and his eyes gaze at the crackling embers of the fire. "You are traveling the other side," he said. "You are looking for some-thing."

"Yes," I replied. "I am having trouble seeing the truth of it through all the pain."

He was quiet for a few moments. "Your path is a darkling one, fraught with pain and blood and death," he said, giving echo to my thoughts. "Any person would have trouble seeing truth in the midst of that."

"Should I cease my search?" I asked.

His eyes snapped to mine. "No," he said. "Though I think you are missing something vital. All that pain, and blood, and death...all that misery...has a point, a purpose. Much of it has been wrought to serve that purpose."

"Wrought by whom?

He looked as though I should know the answer to that question, and like he was holding something back. I raised my eyebrows at him. "By...by *you*," he said.

I rocked back as if I had been slapped. Me?

Gweilt's eyes went back to the fire as he continued to speak. "Do not mistake my words, please," he said. "I do not mean that you created the evil circumstances that necessitated all that violence. I mean that the evil rose, and you *answered* it with violence. As was your right. As was necessary to stop it. Your actions have given back uncounted stolen lives. Stopped the most nefarious of evils cold. Created the potential for an enormous amount of good."

He looked at me directly again and placed a hand on my shoulder. "You are one of the few who has sought out the means to bring death, fettered only by your will, to this world, to hunt down and remove those who perpetrate evils upon their fellow humans. Of those few who have sought this terrible power, you have retained your humanity. You are a good man, Lugh. I am proud to know you, and grateful to be able to call you brother."

I nodded, my eyes welling with tears. "Why am I struggling to understand a path that I chose?" I asked.

He was quiet while he looked at me, searching my eyes. Then he said, "You are not struggling to understand the path. You are struggling to accept the cost it exacts from you."

I looked back to the fire. "The cost," I said.

"Yes," Gweilt responded. "The cost of your chosen path is particularly heavy. All warriors are haunted by the lives they have taken, regardless of how horrible the enemy may be. A human life is a human life, and deliberately ending a life exacts a toll upon one's soul. Men and women fighting for a good and noble cause may only take a single life during the course of a war, but the cost of doing so may utterly destroy their spirit." He paused, removing his hand from my shoulder and looking back to the fire.

"Death is never pretty, my friend," he said. "It always touches more than the one it is visited upon. Taking a single life, even in defense of one's self, home and family, can be destructive in the extreme. You...." He looked back to me, his voice dropping lower. "You have taken *thousands*."

My hands flew to cover my face, and I sobbed. "Thousands?" I asked, guts wrenching.

Gweilt's voice came to me through a fog of weeping. "All of them were justified, brother. You are struggling only because you have forgotten the reason why you did what you did. You are having trouble justifying your actions because you do not remember how this path started."

He put his hand back on my shoulder, and I felt a gentle pressure as he squeezed. I looked at him and met his eyes again. "Stay strong, brother," he said. "Answers will come. You are seeking absolution for the path you have walked, the path you continue to walk. You seek salvation because you do not yet understand that you have *been* salvation for those who could not defend themselves against the evils of men who came to do them harm. Because you feel the cost of the path, but do not yet realize the good it has wrought."

I nodded, getting myself back under control. I swiped at my eyes. "The good?" I asked.

"Something for you to consider," Gweilt said. "Taking a life exacts a terrible toll on a person. *Saving a life* does far more to pay that debt than anything else. Yes, you have taken thousands of lives. But in doing so, you have *saved* far more than that." He smiled lightly. "Your debt was repaid as soon as it was incurred, and then some. The young lives you save create *generations* of good."

I stopped sobbing completely then. Could it be true?

"You have two more destinations left in your seeking, I think," he said. He placed his fingertips on my forehead and said, "You will find peace, brother. A little more sadness and violence, and then you will see. I bid you a merry parting, and merry we will meet again."

I closed my eyes as he pressed his fingertips against my forehead.

# Chapter Nineteen

I woke up…again. For a few moments, I had no idea where I was. It was cold. Through the log walls around me, I could hear the howling of wind. So, I was in a cabin again. I sat up and looked around.

The small cabin was sparse and almost barren. A small and simple hearth, a single chair, a basic bedroll of animal hides…the place was almost empty. There were a lot of…well, I suppose it would be charitable to call them "journals." Scraps and sheets of paper were scattered across the place, haphazardly stacked in corners and bundled into sheaves and rolls. Despite being empty of furniture, the place was…chaotic. It was a mess.

This disturbed me. A lot. Aside from obviously being my home, this was also the den of a man in the grip of consuming madness. Seriously.

I got up from the bedroll and went to the hearth, kindling a small fire there to ward off the bitter chill. Then I sat down in the chair and picked up a small stack of papers. It seemed there wasn't much to do here except read, so I started reading.

The first page had references to the goddess Hel and the god Baldur. It also contained several references to death and resurrection. This page was all about how to bring someone back from death. So was the next one. And the one after that. I searched through other piles and scraps. They all shared the same theme: how to bring someone back. They also shared the same conclusion: it wasn't going to happen.

My hands started shaking, and I felt the pull of the madness. I *must* find an answer to this.

Who was I trying to bring back?

My head seemed to split. It was incredibly painful. I grasped my head in my hands and let out a semi-stifled scream of agony. What was happening to me?

I didn't get a chance to contemplate. A pounding knock upon my door startled me to my feet and I grabbed my sword out of its sheath. "Who is it?" I shouted. I couldn't hear the reply, but I could tell it was a woman's voice. I strode quickly to the door and pulled it open just enough to peek through. Against a field of solid white, a young woman with braided hair of gold stood. She was obviously an adult, tall and slender and – beneath the cold weather clothing

– well-muscled. She was also standing on a pair of skis, long and broad and barely sunken into the white powder that coated the ground. I pulled the door open wider and stared at her cold gray eyes. "I did not hear," I said. "Who are you?"

"My name is Fallon," she replied. I noticed she had a wolf with her, sitting in the snow beside her and shivering slightly with the cold. Despite this, it did not move. "I am seeking the assistance of the death dancer," she said. She looked me over from head to foot, and her face wrinkled slightly. "Are you...him?" Apparently, I looked less than composed.

"Allow me a guess," I said. "Someone has taken your children."

Her face went slack for a moment as though she didn't believe what she was hearing. "Not mine," she said. "My sister's."

I sighed and made a welcoming gesture. It wasn't much of a guess, given the running theme of my experiences of late. It was still disconcerting. She stepped out of the skis and stepped up to my door. I gestured to the wolf as well, and he stepped up beside her. "Be welcome to my hall, Fallon...and your compatriot." They walked in past me, and I shut the door.

The wolf promptly curled up in front of the fire, lying down. Fallon stood still, looking around at the admittedly messy cabin. I walked back to the chair and cleared it, putting my sword back in its sheath.

"Please," I said, gesturing to the chair, "sit down and I will make some tea."

She sat in the chair, still looking around. I walked to the hearth and started making herbal tea, something that would combat the chill. "Tell me what happened," I said softly.

She did, speaking a litany of horrors in a monotone voice. Her composure began to crack at a particularly horrific portion of the story, but I didn't acknowledge it. I got the sense that she would not appreciate my noticing, and it would not do her any good to point out a moment of weakness. I just listened. When the tea was ready, I took her a cup. She took it gratefully and finished with, "In addition to my nephews, they took several other children. They also had several others already. I have no idea why they did this, or who they were." She took a sip of the tea and relaxed just a little bit. "Thank you for the tea," she said.

She seemed to notice her relaxation and said stiffly, "It is *just tea*, right?"

I smiled and held up both hands in a placating gesture. "Just tea," I said. Something occurred to me, and glancing over at Fallon, it was confirmed. She was terrified, but not just of the events she had lived through over the past day and night. She was glancing around the room like a prey animal cornered by predators. She was scared to be *here. She was afraid of me.*

I spoke more softly so as not to startle her. "You called me 'death dancer' when you came to my door," I said. She looked at me sharply, her eyes wide. I slowly raised my hands to show her I meant her no harm and said, "I took no offense. I am merely curious. Do you mind telling me what you know about me?"

She looked around the cabin again, as though watching out for danger. "I have heard many things, but I do not know the truth of them," she said.

Stories were told about me, then. "Perhaps I can offer you some truth," I said.

She tried a smile, but it was strained. Her whole body was tense. I considered a moment and realized that this young woman had literally just skied up to the door of the local crazy boogeyman and brought a problem with her. Now she was sitting in his creepy, messy cabin with him, drinking what she hoped was just normal tea, and her only point of reference were scary stories. Not to mention that I had answered my door with a naked sword and probably looking as crazy as a bag full of cats. Then I had "guessed" her problem involved abducted children.

Well...I felt a little dumb. No wonder she was afraid. She was smart.

"Fallon," I said softly, "I mean you no harm. I apologize for answering my door that way. I was simply startled."

She let out a hefty sigh, and her shoulders slumped a little. She closed her eyes, collecting herself, then nodded. She took another sip of tea and relaxed further. "The stories I have heard are...strange. Some say you conjure spirits. Some say you are an ancient demon. They call you the death dancer because – as the stories tell it – you are one who has learned to dance with blades so well that Death himself follows you to collect the fallen in your path. Some say that you are a poisoner and a...*taikuri.*"

Several things tumbled into place all at once. That last word was Finnish. The snow outside was deep enough that she needed skis to get here. Those two things in combination meant we were in an area known as the Lapland: the far northern reaches of Finland that touch the Arctic circle. She looked like a Laplander, down to her clothing.

I was a Laplander, too...and she had heard that I was a very deadly sorcerer. Was it true? I looked around at all the papers scattered around the cabin, all of them sharing a common theme. It seemed like I was trying to bring someone back that I had lost. So, the whole "conjuring spirits" thing was probably true. That meant the sorcerer part was probably true also, since conjuring spirits and all the associated magics were their purview.

An ancient demon? A poisoner? No. That wasn't me.

I couldn't speak to the "death dancer" thing, though that sounded particularly ominous.

"Uhh...I am definitely not a demon or a poisoner," I said. I tried a weak smile.

She stared at me for a moment, meeting my eyes. Then she *laughed*. She threw her head back and gave a rich, hearty belly laugh. It was enough to make me laugh, too. Even the wolf in front of the hearth lifted his head and let his jaw drop open and his tongue loll out. We laughed a good measure. It was undeniably good for all of us.

"My apologies," Fallon said. "I should know that rumors and stories are not always true."

"No need to apologize," I replied, still chuckling. "I am clearly a little crazy. Look at this place."

She chuckled again and wiped at her eyes. "Perhaps you should conjure some brownies to help with that."

That set us both off again. Brownies were little Fae that were fastidious about cleanliness. She was saying I should consider summoning housekeepers. It was funny.

When the laughing had subsided, I decided it was time to pop the happy bubble we had created. We were both enjoying the respite from the harsh nature of reality, but there was a job to be done...and the lives of children were on the line. As soon as the words were out of my mouth, I hated myself for them.

"You must remember something of them," I said.

Fallon's demeanor changed immediately. The smile vanished, as did the light of humor in her eyes. She bowed her head and shook it, her entire body tense again. "Other than the fact they were men, no." She seemed to remember something, cocked her head to one side, and said, "I do have a token one of them carried." She put a hand into a pocket and produced a leather thong necklace with a bronze emblem hanging from it. "I took this from one of them that I killed, but they took his body."

I held out my hand, and she passed it over to me. The bronze medallion was a simple insignia, and not one I was familiar with. Still, I had a feeling it would be enough.

Fallon asked, "Will that help at all?"

"Fallon," I said, "this is better than any memory." I turned around and walked to the hearth. "How long since you took this?"

"I took it yesterday, about this time," she said. "That was when they attacked."

I noticed the dried blood on the emblem and the strand of leather. "This blood...is it his?" I asked.

"Yes," she said. I looked at her and asked if she was sure about that. "Well," she replied, "I did not decapitate anyone else." Her expression was serious, both eyebrows raised as if to emphasize that statement with the unspoken word "dullard."

Yikes. Note to self: do not cross this woman. Ever. My own expression must have betrayed my thoughts. Her lips had quirked up at one corner. *Oookaay. Down to business.*

I said, "This next part might be somewhat disturbing to you. Please sit in the chair and keep your wolf next to you. Do not speak or draw any attention to yourself. If it helps, you may close your eyes." After a pause, I said, "That may be the best thing you can do."

She didn't ask any questions or make any fuss. She collected her wolf, sat in the chair, and closed her eyes.

I scraped a little of the dried blood into an incense holder and set it on the hearth before the fire. An ethereal woman's voice came to me within a few heartbeats, before I could even begin my summoning. "Honestly, child. You have tried this practice many times, and many times I have told you: I do not have them."

I took a knee, because that's what you do when Hel herself shows up for a chat. "I seek another this time, whose blood I provide for your convenience," I said, and gestured at the incense burner. I wanted so badly to ask who she had referred to but did not dare chance her ire. "He is recently belated, and I must locate his companions."

A few moments passed in silence. I remained on my knee, with my head bowed. After a relative eternity the voice answered, "He is beyond my grasp. Condemned by the Allfather himself to Niflheim, as punishment for the harms he has done to children."

I had to fight to keep my silence, but I did. I squeezed my eyes shut and clenched my fists. If I went to Niflheim to find him, I might never come back. Those children were depending on me.

"Why do you take these matters upon yourself, child?" she asked.

"I can," I replied. I didn't think I needed to explain my choices. To anyone.

"Surely you aware of the toll it exacts from you," Hel said. Her voice sounded almost sad.

"If I must pay a price so that innocent children may live, I do so gladly," I said. "Seeing those children returned safely to their families is reward enough. It is what I have to give, so I will give it."

She seemed to accept that answer and was silent for a few moments more. Then she said, "Your cause is just, though we think the price will be regretfully high in the end. That said, I have acquired a guide to take you to where the children are being held. He will meet you outside when you are ready. I bid you only this warning, child: this night may cost your life."

"Done," I said without hesitation.

There was a soft rushing sound, as though of wind passing, and the flames in the hearth guttered. She was gone. I stood and walked past Fallon, who was looking stricken.

"Do you have your weapons with you?" I asked her.

She nodded and said, "Yes."

"Get them, and make ready to go," I said. She did.

When we were both ready to go, I opened the door and stepped out with Fallon and her wolf behind me. The world was a field of solid white, snow covering everything and blowing fiercely across my vision. I walked through the field of white toward my horse's shelter.

We arrived in the small barn, and my horse – a monstrously large black charger stallion – greeted us with a snort and a bow of his head. As he did this, I saw our guide: a raven sat upon his back.

My confidence shot up. We were going to get those kids back and put an end to this scourge. The Allfather had sent us a guide to make sure we could find them, and I knew I had the skills to make sure the raiders would never do this again. No matter what it cost me.

"Hello, good raven," I said.

Fallon looked at me like I was crazy for talking to a bird – I couldn't blame her – and then gave a startled yelp as the raven replied, "Hello, old friend." She looked at the raven incredulously, and he ducked his head in a nod to her. She returned the nod nervously, never taking her eyes off him.

The raven turned his gaze back to me and said, "I have already shared the location you seek with your horse, along with the fastest route to it, but it is good you brought a wolf. He can guide you more ably than I." He fluttered down to the ground in front of the wolf and...well, *spoke* to him, I suppose. There were some strange bird sounds, and what looked like a complicated little dance. The wolf cocked his head one way, then the other, his ears standing straight up, then gave a little *chuff* sound. I shook my head, and so did Fallon. "Do not worry," said the raven. "He understands."

Fallon looked slowly to me, and I nodded. She looked back to the raven, who said, "I was talking about your wolf." He jerked his beak in my direction. "That one does not have a clue what either of us said."

I balked, outed by the raven. Fallon gave a short bark of laughter and glanced at me. That raven had his beak open and a snarky little light in his eyes. He was laughing at me, too. Even the wolf had a slack-jawed, lolling-tongued look, and my horse gave a whinny. Well, perhaps I deserved that. I smiled bashfully and shrugged.

"Time to go?" I asked.

"Time to go," the raven echoed. "Let the wolf and horse guide their own steps and you will arrive more quickly." He considered a moment, then added, "If I may make a suggestion, I recommend that Fallon stay away from the main conflict. She is an able warrior, but she will do more good – for you and the innocents – from a rear-guard position." He looked directly at Fallon and said, "He will do what is needed, but will not walk away from this fight. You will bring them all home." Fallon and I exchanged a long look, then nodded to the raven.

We mounted the horse and followed the wolf outside in a rush of hooves.

There is a big difference between riding a horse under your guidance and riding a charger that guides himself. Guiding a horse with reins is generally a rough ride, even if the horse is well disciplined. Think about it for a moment from the horse's perspective: somebody with not a clue how you usually move sitting on your back, constantly shifting weight, yanking at your head to tell you when and which direction to turn. If you're really good at running, though, and free to choose your own footing....

The snowy ground, trees, and sky flashed past us in a rush. The well-muscled horse's body moved like a perfect machine, and the ride was extremely smooth. It was like flying. Fallon held tightly to me, but I could just feel her exhilarated smile. I joined her with my own smile. Might as well enjoy the ride.

I thought to myself as the landscape flashed past. This woman was strong, practically fearless, and beautiful. She was fiercely loyal to her family and had a deep well of love for her own. She was somebody I would be honored to call my wife. I was stunned. I had not allowed myself to consider that possibility before, since...since...since I had lost my wife and daughter. The image of the woman and little girl standing in front of the log home slapped me in the face like a brick. It hurt like a brick, too. I gasped.

They were the ones I was obsessed with bringing back. Loved ones I had lost.

I could have loved this woman. Could have led a happy life with her. Could have had children, and other family members. I could have been happy. I had made a choice to linger in the past, and it had kept me from enjoying the most basic things about life. Now, it was too late. My path, my fate, was fixed. I could not do anything now to earn this woman's love except save the missing children...and I had been told, quite clearly, that doing so would, inevitably, lead to my death. A single tear streamed down my cheek, and I ignored it.

*So be it.*

My features firmed as I let my eyes drift closed and played out the looming battle in my mind.

When I opened my eyes, we had stopped moving. We were just behind the tree line of an old-growth forest that fronted on a large open expanse of snowy ground. We were on a rise above the flat ground, where a fortified building stood. It wasn't enormous, but it was large enough. It was also surrounded with a log palisade. The gates facing us were the only way in or out.

I felt Fallon let go of me and dismount the horse. I followed her. We both walked to the edge of the tree line, looking at the fortress. "How do we get in there?" she asked quietly.

"*We* do not," I replied. "I will get them to come out." She started to argue, but I shook my head once and cut her off. "I have already made my choice. I will get them to come out, and I will fight them." I looked at her gray eyes, and said, "I need you to climb that tree with your bow and all the arrows and cover my back. Shoot only when it is absolutely necessary. Do *not* be seen."

She returned my gaze with tear tracks on her cheeks and a solid, stubborn stance. She looked like she wanted to protest, fervently, but she nodded. She kept my gaze for another few heartbeats, and then she turned back to the horse and gathered her bow and both quivers of arrows. She walked to the tree I had indicated and began to climb.

I watched her go up the tree until she was settled on a thick branch, my heart breaking at the thought of what might have been. My choices had lead me here. Time to finish it. I turned and began walking down to the heavy gates.

I walked across the empty ground before the fortress gates slowly and deliberately. The only good reasons for placing a fortress on cleared ground was that you could see an enemy coming, that you could deny the enemy cover and concealment, and that you could destroy them before they reached your gates. I *wanted* them to see me. I *wanted* them to know that I was approaching their gates, and that I was alone. I *wanted* them to know that one man was slowly and deliberately approaching their gates. After all, I *wanted* them to see no threat.

I walked right up to those gates and pounded on them with both fists. I belted out a loud, crazed shout, "You took my children!"

A crazed father, perhaps drunk, seeking vengeance? The role was easy enough to play, and now I knew why. I had worn this costume before.

After a few minutes, and a little more stagecraft that convinced even me, the gates opened on three men armed with swords. A fourth man, also with a sword, stepped in front of them and replied, "We have no children here. Who told you this?"

"My source of information is beyond reproach," I said. "You have many children here, and none of them are yours. I will have them back."

The fourth man stepped toward me, and his guards stepped forward with him. "You will leave now."

I gave him a lopsided grin.

"Will I?" I asked with a little taunting tone to my voice. "I think it will take a lot more than the four of you. I think it will take every man in this paltry little fort to make me leave. Why not bring them all out and let us see?" I took a weak, shuffling step forward and looked the man up and down as though sizing him up.

The man looked at me like I was crazy. *Good*, I thought. *Indulge me and bring them all out to "watch." Entertainment is cheap, after all.*

He shoved me back, and I let myself stumble backwards. He turned his back to me and began walking back into the fort. I laughed. He stopped and turned around. "You want to know how I know this is the right place?" I choked out through genuine chuckles. "You arrogant fools put your little sigil on your front gates, and then wander around dropping your tokens of membership when you lose your heads." I reached into my pocket and pulled out the brass emblem on its bloodstained leather thong. I held it up for them all to see and laughed some more. I jangled it a little bit and let my laugh turn taunting in the extreme. "You want this back, do you not? Why not indulge a small personal wager? Call out all of your warriors, and if any of them kill me, you can take it back and throw my body under the ice as food for hungry bears." I tucked the necklace back into my pocket and patted it.

The commander of their guard looked at me with quiet fury. "And if you win?"

"If I win," I said, "there will not be a solitary one of you left alive to worry those children anymore."

His fury boiled over, predictably. He spun back to the gates and gave a snarling shout. Another thirty-six men stepped into view, armed with swords, daggers, and spears. They all stepped up behind their commander, who drew his own blade.

I stood up straight and removed my coat and shirt. The cold of the icy night was bracing. I noticed that my torso was *covered* with scars. I closed my eyes, took a deep breath, and opened them as I drew my sword. I let out my breath with a simple whisper of, "Allfather, guide my blade."

Most people, when they think of fights, think of superiority in terms of numbers. One guy against 40 seems like bad odds. There are a lot of reasons this is simply not true. Generally speaking, people assume larger numbers of enemies means that they will have to defeat all of those enemies *at once*. Those people are forgetting one simple fact: surface area.

Imagine a single man, standing upright. Surround that man with enemies, in a circle close enough to be within arm's reach. You might be able to squeeze six people in there; eight if you don't allow them to actually move their arms, which completely defeats the purpose. Even with fists, four would be a serious liability, even if they were well coordinated. Now put swords, daggers and spears in their hands. Suddenly, everybody has to stand at a different distance based on what weapon they're holding: daggers cannot hit the target outside arm's reach, and spears are useless and cumbersome in close quarters. When two enemies attack a single combatant with long weapons, it is not uncommon their blades will cross and interfere with each other. That possibility rises exponentially with each additional enemy you introduce.

Now assume the guy in the center of that circle knows how to read combat actions and participants like a simple book. Add to that the assumption that the guy in the middle can *move*.

The 40 men attacked me in a swarm, and I began to *dance*. There's not a better way to describe it. The crunching of snow, the whistle of cloven air, the shouts and grunts, the ringing of steel: all of them came to me as a kind of living music that painted a picture of the evolving battle in my mind. I danced, blade whirling. It was not as much a fight as it was a carefully choreographed execution. I danced. They died. It was all over in a matter of minutes.

I looked down at myself and saw a bunch of bruises and cuts, but nothing lethal. I waved my gore-coated sword overhead to catch Fallon's attention and let her know it was safe to approach.

I felt a piercing sting in the right side of my back, then my chest. I looked down and saw a bloody arrowhead and shaft protruding from the right side of my chest. My legs buckled, and I collapsed to my knees. I coughed, and blood erupted from my mouth.

I heard a whistle as an arrow passed me and I heard a grunt from the archer who had taken me. I had made a fatal mistake, and it was born of simple arrogance. These men were cowards...and cowards never charge headlong into battle when they have another option.

Fallon came running up to me through the snow and dropped the bow as she dropped to her knees in front of me to help. I shook my head fiercely and gasped, "The children. Get the children out of there." She nodded, stood, drew her own sword, and ran into the fortress.

I knelt in the snow, trying not to move too much, trying to keep my breathing steady. I heard Fallon come out with a bunch of crying children and give a loud, sharp whistle. I heard the soft thunder of my horse's hooves as he came galloping up. I reached up to the arrow shaft, held it steady with one hand, and snapped off the head. I screamed, and a lot of blood came out with the sound. I screamed again when Fallon yanked the arrow shaft out of my back. More blood came out of my mouth. The world got blurry.

"Are they safe?" I asked.

Fallon nodded, and then spoke softly, "Yes. They are all safe."

I felt someone pressing cloth to my chest and back, tying something around my chest, and then replacing my shirt and coat. The world faded to black.

I woke, briefly, to a startling scene. I was back in my cabin. Fallon was kneeling before the small hearth, speaking to...I couldn't believe my eyes. She was speaking to an older man. He was tall, with long iron hair and beard, and a patch over one eye. Could it be...?

I heard the man say, "I am sorry, Fallon. His own choices lead him here, and I will not undo his free will – will not dishonor him – by changing his fate. It grieves me to see him broken again, as it will grieve me many more times. Prepare him a pyre, and he will return to you in time."

I closed my eyes.

When I opened them again, I was standing next to a tree outside my cabin. I was looking at a large pile of wood. I no longer felt pain. I no longer felt any physical sensation. I looked up at the tree, and saw the raven sitting on a low branch. He said softly, "This is your seeking, and we thought it would do you some good to see this." He turned his eyes to me and continued, "It is difficult to understand one's own choices, and this will give you some measure of peace."

I heard music and singing and turned back to the scene. Out of the tree line came a procession of people walking in two columns. Some were people from the nearby village. Some were people I did not know. They were all adults. Behind them came the children. They were also walking in two columns. As they reached the neatly stacked pile of wood their paths diverged, and they circled around it. The children formed an inner circle, standing a little closer to the pile of wood than their parents. Some of the children obviously didn't have parents there, but they did not stand alone. They stood with other children, with other families.

The last six children were carrying a plank on their shoulders. It wasn't ornate or extravagant, just a simple wooden plank. I was lying on top of it. They placed the plank – and me – atop the pile of wood and stood back with the other children. Then I noticed the last person in the line. It was Fallon. Her face was streaked with tears. She walked slowly up to the pile of wood, climbed up enough to lean over me, and planted a gentle kiss upon my forehead. I heard her whisper to me as though I were inside my body. "There were nearly a hundred children held captive at that place," she said. "They were going to be sacrificed or sold into slavery. You saved them. All of them are here. Your death was not in vain. We will remember you. Thank you."

She stepped down and knelt at the base of the funeral pyre, working with a couple of pieces of flint. The funeral pyre took light, and within a few seconds my body was engulfed in flames. Fallon took the hands of the two children closest to her – her nephews, I assumed – and they took the hands of the children next to them...all the way around the circle. Then the same thing happened with the adults.

"Each of those children lived good lives, now and in what you would call their future...future lives, that is," said the raven. "Some took in orphans, some pursued and punished those who harm children, and some still participate in or give to charitable organizations. Immeasurable good came out of this."

"Really?" I asked.

"Truly," replied the raven. "I know you are having considerable trouble with the...time...thing, so I will not complicate it further for you. However, consider the Viking funeral ritual of placing a revered Chieftain in a boat and pushing it out into a fjord while it burns. Why do you think they did that?"

"To signify his travel to the afterlife?" I asked.

"In part, that is true," replied the raven. "The boat is a means of transport, and the fire is a means of transformation. However, the boat makes ripples as it travels across the water. Those little ripples are the important part."

"You mean that what we do in our short mortal lives has an influence on what comes after we are gone," I said.

The raven nodded. "The ritual is symbolic," he said. "A fjord is open to the sea, and that sea touches every shore of every continent in this world. A small ripple has the potential to become a wave, then a tidal force. The only symbolic flaw in that ritual is the chieftain."

I looked a question at the raven.

"Not only a chieftain has this simple and potent power," he said. "All human beings have the same power to influence the world beyond their lifetimes. Some do it through raising children to carry on their legacy. Others do it by influencing their compatriots or giving of themselves to organizations that will outlive them. Some use their knowledge and creativity to invent things that help or hurt people. Some simply keep to themselves. All of these have an influence."

I considered that and remained silent.

"This is part of the true beauty of creation," the raven said. "A beauty that most miss. Humans dream of immortality, they pray for it, and some devote their entire lives to attaining it. The problems of mortal flesh are persistent: physical pleasure, hunger, shelter, thirst, and the longing for power to guarantee those other needs are met have never been defeated by humanity. They are not meant to be defeated. They are a proving ground."

I began to understand just how out of my depth I was. "A proving ground?"

The raven continued by asking me a question. "How can you be cherished – or punished – for eternity...if you are only mortal?"

"I...I...." I couldn't bring myself to say it.

"How could you experience all these many lifetimes full of joy, pain, and all the rest, if you were merely perishable?" The raven looked at me directly. "The answer to these questions is quite simple," he said. "It is one of the most fundamental truths of your existence."

I steeled myself and met the raven's gaze before answering. "I...*we*...were created immortal," I said. "If mortal bodies are perishable, but I persist, then I am not a body with a soul. I am a soul with a body."

"A simple but important distinction," said the raven.

The revelation struck me like a stick to the nose. "We were created as immortal souls," I said. "We are born into the mortal world to learn...to live through the problems of mortal flesh to learn...*something*."

"You would call it true happiness," the raven said. "Contentedness is possibly a better word for it. The ability to be content with any circumstance."

I balked. "Really?"

The raven cocked his head to one side and stated, "You have not considered this."

"Well, I have, but...." I had considered the old maxim "be happy with what you have" many times, but it never seemed to be...enough. Well, crap. There it was. It never seemed to be "enough."

"Exactly," said the raven.

"So...Heaven is a reflection of your own personal happy place?" I asked.

The raven seemed to consider this. "More accurately, Heaven is what you make it. As is Hell."

Two things about this rocked me back on my heels. First, his use of Christian terms. Second, the notion that the afterlife – good and bad – was *malleable*. "You mean we choose where we go."

"In a manner of speaking," the raven replied. "However, this is not part of your seeking. The answers you seek about the afterlife are not answers I can give you. You seek the truth about the Divine."

"Are the two not related?" I asked.

The raven moved his wings in an imitation of a shrug. "They are," he said, "and they are not."

I sighed and stood in silence for a long while, then said softly, "I do not understand."

The raven said just as softly, "That is why you are here. It is also why I have been appointed as your guide. What better guide to truth than memory?"

"I will follow you," I said.

"No," the raven replied. "You follow yourself."

Wait. What?

"Over the course of your many mortal lifetimes," he continued, "you have created only one child. How did you do it?"

An image of the little girl petting a chicken flashed through my mind. "My daughter," I said. "What do you mean by your question?"

"I do not refer to the physical act," he said sardonically. "I am too well acquainted with the metaphor of the birds and the bees."

I...chuckled. I couldn't help it. The raven joined me.

"I mean to say," the raven continued, "that the act of creation requires one to give of himself."

"I understand," I said. "The male and female both contribute physical components to create a new life."

"Yes," he responded. "Though that is only the physical. Much more goes into creating a new being. Hopes. Dreams. Love. All of these, and more, are contributed by the parents of a new being."

You would think I had grown tired of being hit in the face with invisible revelations. You would be wrong. I gasped. "We...are...children...."

The raven nodded. "Now you see," he said. "You are *much* more than mere flesh and bone." He paused long enough for me to hear the continued singing around my funeral pyre. "You are now ready to finish the memory that began this seeking. I suggest that you have one more conversation with your friend Tim before continuing, however."

"I will," I said.

The raven nodded and said, "Time to wake up."

# Chapter Twenty

I awoke with a startled gasp and found myself back in my apartment. Dawn had not broken yet, but I remembered that it was Saturday and felt relieved I had a free day. Hopefully, Tim was game for more coffee and conversation.

I spent my morning cleaning my apartment and clothes. I called Tim in the early afternoon, and he suggested a local bar in lieu of the coffee shop. We were both into Texas music – a genre dubiously dubbed "Americana" – and the local bar was hosting a local favorite. I agreed to meet him at eight, and he said he was bringing tacos. If you haven't experienced this combo, you're missing out.

We met up at the cozy little bar and found a small picnic table on the back patio. I provided a pitcher of good, dark beer and two pint glasses. He provided a veritable feast of tacos. For a while, we just ate and drank and enjoyed the music.

"Well," he said, leaning back from the bag of taco wrappers and taking up a freshly filled pint. "How's things?"

I filled up my own pint glass, remaining silent until I had taken a few swallows. I had a good idea who this man was, and I was pretty sure his name wasn't "Tim." But should I let him know that I knew? I decided the best course of action was to simply have a conversation.

"I've been thinking a lot about our last conversation, and I have some questions," I said.

He smiled. "I thought you might," he said.

I nodded and smiled in turn. "I'll just jump right into it, shall I?"

"Please," he said, displaying two open palms. "You're buying the beer, after all."

I laughed, though it was a bit strained. This was going to be like stepping off a high cliff into a bottomless pit with a blindfold covering my eyes. I took another drink. Nothing for it but to jump. Might as well get on with it.

"I got the impression that the Old Norse deities were our ancestors, not gods and goddesses," I said.

Tim nodded.

"I also got the impression that they were given the label of deities much later, by the people who wrote down the old tales," I said.

He nodded again.

I continued, "I recently heard the theory that we are all created as immortal souls, and that we are all children of the Creator."

Tim actually laughed. "Theory, huh? That's a theory, is it?"

I lifted my eyebrows. "Is it not?" I asked.

"Sorry," Tim said, still chortling. "You may call that a theory, but it seems like cold logic to me."

"I presume you buy it then," I said. "Mind sharing your thoughts?"

Tim took another drink, draining his glass, and looked at me with that same knowing smile. "Why don't you share yours, and I'll just jump in when I see fit," he said. "This is your journey, after all. I'm just a spectator."

That last bit was about all the confirmation I needed. My hand shook as I picked up my glass and took another drink.

"Let's say I believe it," I said. "The Creator put a bit of himself into the first humans, and they passed it on to their children, and so on down the line to us. Wouldn't that make us all....?"

Tim burst into laughter again and said, "Hardly. Even if we got our little piece of divinity directly from the Creator, that would still be a tiny piece. It doesn't make us any more a god than the skills we learn." He took another drink of the dark beer, and with a pleased sigh said, "Though I wouldn't doubt the Alebrewer has been passing out some trade secrets."

"Alright," I said, shaking my head. "Alright, I'm a little baffled. You're saying that we are all *semi-divine*."

Tim nodded, encouraging me to continue.

"That makes no sense," I said.

"It makes perfect sense," Tim replied. "There are clues all over the place."

"I must have missed them," I said.

"More likely," Tim said, "you have just failed to recognize them for what they are, like everybody else." He looked over the rim of his glass at me. "The funny part is that they're right in front of you."

I sat silently, waiting for him to continue.

"You should at least read the gospel," Tim said with a sigh. "In the book of John, when Jesus is going to be stoned for blasphemy, he reminds the Jews that their own law says, 'you are gods.' We are made in God's image. Ever heard the little kids' song that goes, 'This little light of mine?'"

Stunned, I just sat there. He was right. There were tons of references to this kind of thing. All over the place.

"So, our ancestors...." I trailed off, trying to think it through.

"Were just ancestors," Tim finished for me. At my startled face, he held up his hands in a conciliatory gesture. "That doesn't mean that they were any less majestic than the stories make them out to be," he said. "Just that they were human like us."

"That, specifically, makes absolutely no sense," I said.

"Why not?" Tim asked.

"Well..." I said. "If they were human like us, and even half the stories are true...."

Tim lifted his eyebrows in question.

"Well, look," I said. "I can't make lightning strike and thunder rumble. I don't understand the mysteries of the runes. I can't shape-shift or make magical weapons or...well, any of that stuff."

"Really?" asked Tim. "How do you know?"

I just stared at him, my face a mask, waiting for him to laugh at me.

"Have you tried?" he asked.

"Go ahead," I said. "Admittedly, it's funny. Go ahead and laugh." I took a long drink.

Now Tim looked confused. "Who said I was joking?"

"You must be," I said.

"Why?" he asked.

"Because it's ridiculous!" I said.

"So," he said, "you say you can't, and you regard it as such a ridiculous notion that you haven't even tried." He considered this a moment as he topped off both our glasses from the pitcher. "Seems to me that the only thing in your way is yourself." He put the empty pitcher back on the table with a solid thunk.

I couldn't respond to this. I just didn't know what to say.

"You believe that those who came before you could do these things, but for some reason you believe yourself...*less*...than them," Tim said. "That is your biggest problem."

I took another drink, trying to think of something to say. He was right, of course. I did think of myself as less than my ancestors. I thought about it. There was a long list of reasons why I thought of myself this way. My grandfathers had both been veterans of horrible wars. One of them was a rancher who could feed his family without visiting a grocery store, and frequently did, by hunting, fishing, and gardening. My great grandparents on that same side of the family had lived entirely off the land their whole lives. I wasn't sure I could do the same, much less call down the lightning or anything so grandiose. Then again...I hadn't tried.

Sure, I had proven that I could survive in the wilderness with no more than a knife. I had a reasonable idea of how to cultivate my own fruits and vegetables from helping my grandmother in her garden. I could hunt. I could fish. I could find or build shelter. I knew how to purify water for cooking or drinking. I was a reasonably accomplished swordsman and archer. In fact, I knew how to *make* a knife, sword, spear, bow, and arrows from raw materials. But I couldn't....

...could I?

I looked up to find Tim smiling again, waiting patiently for me to think it through. "Now," he said, "you're asking the right question." He glanced at his watch, drained his glass, and stood. "I need to get home," he said. "It's late."

I stood and shook his hand. "Thank you," I said.

He smiled again and winked. "My genuine pleasure, brother," he said. "You're an interesting guy, and smarter than the average bear."

I laughed, and we parted ways.

When I got back to my apartment, the raven was sitting perched on the footboard of my bed.

# Chapter
# Twenty-One

I opened my eyes on the forest.

It looked like late evening, and I had the reins of my horse in one hand. I looked behind the horse and saw a makeshift litter dragging on the ground, a wild boar and a deer laid across it.

I was back in the memory of my wife and daughter, and my hunting was done. My heart gave a joyous leap. I was headed home and would see them again shortly.

A piercing scream split the quiet of the forest like a sharp axe to the guts. That's what it felt like. That scream could only have come from my wife. *Raiders?* I drew my sword and swiftly cut the leads that held the litter in place, then mounted my horse and jabbed my heels into it, bringing it up to a sprint.

When my horse burst from the tree line, my eyes were witness to horror. My home and barn and chicken coop were all on fire. My wife and daughter were nowhere to be seen. Nor was anyone else.

I caught a flicker of movement from the house and stared. It was my wife, her body completely engulfed in flames. I felt a gush of breath escape me as her burned body fell into the ashes and embers and lay motionless.

Tears sprang to my eyes as I hastily dismounted the horse and ran toward the house. The heat of the burning timbers stopped me in my tracks, and I collapsed to my knees. I could do no more than watch, and sob. Was my daughter in there also, burning? I could not see her as I could my wife.

I gasped in surprise when a hand grabbed my shoulder. I spun to face whoever had grabbed me, sinking to my backside in the dirt and bringing my sword up to skewer the person. The man jumped back with a "Whoa!" and raised his hands to show me he wasn't armed. I couldn't see very well through the tears.

"Easy, brother," said the man, still backing away slowly. "Be at ease. We are not here to hurt you."

I recognized the voice as my nearest neighbor's and let the sword drop as I swiped at my eyes. I looked around at the other people assembled there. They were unmistakably the people I had already encountered in my seeking, and in other times I remembered. Liam was there, as was Gweilt...though their names were different in this time. I stared for just a moment before the man – I knew him as Liam – came back to kneel in front of me.

"We were chasing the raiders when we came across you," he said. "They hit each of us in turn earlier today. Stole some livestock and grain and tried for a few of the children, but we were at home and at least discouraged them from that."

Gweilt stepped forward and cleared his throat. Everybody looked at him, and when he caught Liam's eye he gestured to the burning house. Liam looked over the burning wreckage and must have seen my wife's burning body. He let out a groan of dismay and hugged me, saying quietly, "I am sorry, brother. So sorry."

I allowed myself to sob against him for a few moments.

I heard Gweilt clear his throat again and, raising my head from Liam's shoulder, saw him step toward us. He was holding something.

I swiped at my eyes again to clear them and held out my hand to take whatever it was he was now offering out to me. As I took the little thing, I felt a fresh wave of nausea and mourning wash over me like a tidal wave. It was a little wooden chicken I had carved for my daughter a few years ago. She loved the little thing as she loved the real chickens and had even collected some feathers and fixed them to the little wooden doll with a swatch of cloth.

"My daughter..." I croaked out. "Where...?"

"We found the doll by the chicken coop," Gweilt said. "But we found no sign of her."

The chicken coop. The little girl had probably run out to protect them during the raid....

I hung my head, staring at the little wooden chicken, and thought. No sign of my daughter found meant that she may still be alive. I whipped my head up to look at Gweilt and said, "You think they took her."

"Yes," he said.

"Do you know where?"

He shook his head.

With Liam's assistance, I regained my feet and picked up my sword. I sheathed it and looked back to the small group of men. "I will need help to get this done quickly, if you do not mind," I said. They all nodded. I pointed to a large willow tree by the water's edge. "I would like to lay her to rest under that tree." Except for Liam and Gweilt, they all turned and began walking to the tree to dig a grave.

It took the three of us the better part of an hour to retrieve my wife's remains from the ruins of the house, as it was still on fire. I took my time wrapping her body gently in my riding cloak, as everything else we had was burned in the house. The whole sad, gory mess was burned into my mind, and I had a feeling that it would stay there forever.

After we had lowered my wife into the grave and covered her body with earth, I allowed myself a few minutes of quiet mourning. I rose and marked her burial spot with a large, smooth stone. Then I turned to the small group of men and said, "I am going after them. I will get my daughter back, and I will not leave one of them alive. It will be hard, and dangerous, and bloody. I know that some of you have families to look after, and it is likely they are already worried about you. You have all given me great help, and I am in your debt. Please return to your families and farms with my heartfelt thanks."

Everybody left after final handshakes. Everybody except Gweilt and Liam.

"Brothers..." I said.

"Stop," Liam said quietly. "Yes, we have families, and yes, they are worried. But we saw this evening what could have easily happened if we had been away from home. We cannot allow this threat to continue, nor leave an innocent little girl to these monsters."

"We are coming with you," said Gweilt simply.

I nodded, trying to keep my eyes clear. "Thank you," I said.

We rode hard through most of the night, following the sloppy trail left by the raiders. It wasn't difficult, even by moon and starlight. Broken branches, trampled grasses, and earth torn up by their horses' hooves were easy enough to spot from a distance.

We slept for a few hours just before dawn and then continued our pursuit, which had taken us on a rambling course along the shore of the ocean. Our horses were having trouble with the rocky terrain, so we moved inland just enough to ride in forested ground where we could still see the shore.

We rode hard until midday. That's when we saw the people standing at the foot of a high cliff.

It took us a while to find a trail down to the shore from the heights of the cliffs, and we had to abandon the horses halfway down. At the foot of the cliff, several people – probably from the large homestead we had seen at the top, which was also burned – stood in a ragged half-circle, just looking at the shoreline. I could hear soft sobs from some of them, so I slowed my steps. When we were a few paces away, a man turned swiftly toward us with a farming tool and lurched forward, taking a wild swing with it. It was a simple flat hoe, and it almost took my nose off.

I stumbled back and lost my footing, falling on my backside on the wet rocks. Another man, this one older, came forward with a roar and grabbed the hoe out of the younger man's hands, restraining him. "It is not them, fool boy!" shouted the older man. "Those cowards rode away at dawn!"

"We are chasing them," said Liam, his hands raised.

"What happened here?" asked Gweilt, gesturing to the half-circle of people.

I didn't hear the answer. I had caught sight of something that stopped my heart and knocked the breath from my lungs. The lower hem of a simple green dress, and a simple buckskin moccasin. It couldn't be her. I groaned in agony as I regained my feet, saying, "No...please, no...no...."

I pushed through the line of people and saw the thing I had been dreading most since I first heard my wife scream the previous evening. My daughter's small, broken body lay among the rocks. There were several other children lying around her, all of them very obviously dead. I sank to my knees beside her and cradled her sweet golden head in my lap. I stroked her long hair very gently, unable to keep the tears from flowing down my cheeks or the agonized whimpers and wails from escaping my throat. It was too much. I hugged her to me, rocked back and forth, and wept.

I don't know how long I sat there. I vaguely remembered seeing some of the people carry away the other young ones, but it was all in the periphery. I simply could not pry my eyes from the sweet, innocent face of my daughter. It began to rain, but I didn't care. I just sat there on my knees, mourning, trying to memorize every tiny detail: the little freckles on her face and arms from tending to the chickens in the sun, the beautiful blue of her eyes like the sky before a storm, the golden locks that mimicked the color of honey. It was just too much.

I picked up her broken form gingerly to carry her up to the remains of the homestead. When I turned around, Liam and Gweilt were both still standing there, their heads bowed. Neither of them tried to take her from me, to help me, or to even say anything to me. One walked ahead of me and the other behind me, and I had the distinct impression they were protecting me.

They were good men.

When I reached the homestead at the top of the cliff, I approached one of the houses and gently kicked at the door, as I could not use my hands to knock. I stood back from the door a few paces and, when it opened on the older man I had seen when we arrived, I choked out, "My task is not done, and I can spare no more time yet for...."

He nodded and held out his arms. "Your brothers told us what happened, son,"" he said softly. "I will keep her and care for her until you return."

I sobbed a little more, hugging my little girl close to me. I gently kissed her forehead and passed her small form to the old man, who took her with the utmost care and respect. I felt my breath rushing out of me again. "Thank you," I said.

I began walking toward the cliff's precipice, and as I passed Gweilt his hand grasped my arm lightly. "Where are you going, brother?"

I looked him directly in the eyes and said flatly, "To call for help." His eyes widened in something like shock, and his hand let me go and dropped back to his side. I had the impression he could see the hate, the wrath, burning in my heart. "Make ready to leave," I said. "I will not be long. When the moon rises, we will depart."

He said, "Be careful what you ask, brother."

I nodded at him and continued my walk to the edge of the cliff.

I stood right on the edge of the cliff and looked down. Far below, the sharp rocks and surging surf clashed. I looked up at the endless sky and raised my arms. "Odin!" I called out. "Allfather, I seek your counsel!"

The response was immediate and somewhat frightening. A fierce chill wind burst over the face of the cliff and pushed me back a step. I stepped forward again. I would not give in. "If you judge me unworthy of your presence," I said, "you may throw me from this cliff. I will not give in otherwise."

I looked down at the crashing surf, my arms still raised to my sides. When I looked up again, he was standing in front of me. That's right: he was standing in front of me, in mid-air. There was a black eyepatch covering one eye, and a long walking staff in one hand. With his other hand he reached out and put a palm against my chest. He took a couple of steps forward, gently pushing me back from the precipice. I didn't resist. When his feet were on solid ground, I took a knee.

"Stand up, young one," he said. "You are not meek, and I am not one who admires such gestures."

I stood and looked at him. He was tall, but not overly so. He was wearing a long, gray cloak that billowed gently in the breeze. He had long hair and beard, both the color of iron. His face was...well, he looked a little sad.

"I know what you would ask me, lad," he said. "I know the raw hate that burns inside you. I see the grief that permeates your very being. I hear the wails of despair you dare not give voice. I feel your pain, son...but the thing you would ask of me will only add to those ails."

I was quiet for a moment, thinking, then said, "I see it as necessary."

"Oh, it is necessary," Odin said. "Someone must stand against this evil. Someone of your realm. The problem is that this evil is insidious and persistent, rising again with each generation...and I fear that you are not one to let it go. I fear that you will continue to pursue it, and that the cost to yourself will be too much to bear."

I kept my silence for just a few moments more, biting back a hot remark, and said the one thing that seemed to fit. "Whatever the cost, I stand fast."

Odin hung his head, his chin on his chest, and leaned on his staff. "You seek the knowledge to bring death to those who deserve punishment, to remove this evil from Midgard by force. Such knowledge cannot be passed to you by telling a tale. The only able instructor is experience." He reached out his right hand to my forehead. "I ask only that you understand how much this hurts me, to pass on this knowledge to you."

I nodded, and he touched the fingertips of his right hand to my left temple.

I opened my eyes to the nightmare.

Thick darkness, shadowy figures, and fires burning low and dull throughout the valley. I couldn't see the stars.

I tried to walk toward the nearest fire, to get away from the chill that encompassed me. The shadowy figures pressed in around me, blocking my progress. As I touched them, trying to push them aside, a sick feeling shuddered through me. I shoved one forcibly out of my way, felt the sickly tingle of contact with evil shudder through me, and then I saw it: the shadowy figure was holding a smaller figure made of stark white light, tearing it to pieces even as it tried to reassemble itself. It was...an evil person, tearing apart an innocent one. As I watched, dark stains appeared on the smaller light being where there would have been scars from the wounds inflicted on it. The shadowy figure grabbed the small figure of light and began to tear at it again, and I felt rage rise inside me as I had never felt before.

I seized the shadowy figure by the head and gave a sharp, vicious twist. The figure just...dissolved. The little being made of light looked at me, then up, and then gave a little leap and disappeared. I looked up...and saw a single star in the sky.

I looked around at the other shadowy figures. They were each tormenting a small light being. I looked up at the single, tiny star, and understood. If I wanted to see the stars, I would have to free these little beings from their tormentors.

I would see the stars.

I fought my way to the first fire, where I found a shield, then to the next fire, where I found a dagger.

The next fire gave me a sword. Each shadowy figure I encountered died, by my hands or blade. More and more stars appeared in the sky. I continued to fight, the rage inside me redoubling each time I saw a little one in agony. I got better, more efficient and effective, as time went on.

Time is a funny thing, as Rina had told me. It's not linear. It doesn't flow in a tidy straight line. The only moment that matters is *now*.

*Now* lasted for a *long, long time*. Centuries. Millennia. I'm not sure how long I battled the forces of darkness. It felt like *forever* in a single moment.

I opened my eyes with a gasp. Odin was still standing before me. A single tear glimmered on his cheek. "You have the experience now, son, and the terrible knowledge that comes along with it," he said softly. "I can do but one more thing for you." He reached up to the clasp of his cloak, unhooked it, and swept it off his shoulders. He offered it out to me and said, "This cloak may keep you warm on the darkling path you now walk."

I took the cloak in both hands gingerly. My hands were not shaking anymore, though this seemed strange to me. I felt unbelievably calm, considering the violent storm that still raged inside me. Perhaps that was a result of the "training" I had just endured.

The cloak was feather-light, almost insubstantial, and I couldn't feel the weight of it as I settled it across my shoulders.

Odin put his hand on my shoulder and said, "Their camp is only a few hours' hard ride from here, and they outnumber you by far. Follow their trail. Trust your instincts. Remember your training. Rescue the other captives they hold. Do not leave even one of these enemies alive."

"Thank you, Allfather," I said.

He shook his head slowly. "I do not require your thanks, young one, for I have done you no service," he said, "but you do deserve ours." He offered me his hand, and I shook it.

"For what?" I asked.

"It is a heavy mantle you have taken upon yourself, son," he said. "It should have been worn by another, but now that responsibility belongs to you. When you are ready to relinquish it, we will make sure it passes to another. Please do not forget that you have this option...and please do not let the darkness overtake you."

I nodded, and he...well, he just vanished.

The moon was rising over the ocean, so I turned back to the homestead and found Liam and Gweilt leading the horses toward me. They stopped and stared as I approached them. Both of them were staring at the gray cloak.

Liam pointed at it asked, "Where did you get that?"

I shook my head with a small smile.

Gweilt's eyes were wide. "Did you get the help you asked for?"

"Yes," I replied. Gweilt bowed his head to me, which he had never done before. I couldn't help myself and chuckled, saying, "Stop that, brother. I am still myself."

"Are you sure?" he asked, peering at me with a pointed sidelong glance.

I laughed in earnest this time. The man's sidelong, wide-eyed glance was somehow comical. "Completely," I replied, and mounted my horse.

Gweilt shrugged and mounted his own horse. "No point taking chances," he said.

I heard Liam ask Gweilt in a quiet undertone, "Where did he get that gray cloak?"

"Exactly where you think he did," Gweilt answered him in the same tone. "Keep an eye on him. If he starts throwing around runic spells and his horse grows another set of legs, we will know something is afoot."

"Are you serio...?"

I turned to look back at them and they both fell silent, looking back at me. Gweilt glanced sideways at Liam, a small grin threatening to light up his face and give away the joke. "Relax, brothers," I said. "As far as I know, it is only a cloak."

We set off through the night with a hearty laugh. We found the trail easily enough.

---

We found the raiders close to midnight.

They were camped in a large clearing in the forest along both banks of a stream. A makeshift cage of roughly hewn timbers held their captives near the middle of the camp. All of the captives were either young women or children, and there were close to a hundred of them cramped in the cage, huddled close together and unable to even lie down to sleep.

The rage boiled up inside me, and it was all I could do to contain it. I looked at Gweilt and Liam and said, "Free the captives and lead them away to safety as quietly as you can. I will provide a rearguard. Once they are safe, we will return and clean up."

"Clean up?" Gweilt asked.

I turned my gaze back to the enemy camp, quietly drawing my sword. "Not one of them leaves this place alive."

We crept quietly into the camp, and Liam made quick work of the ropes binding the door of the cage shut. The captives were eager to leave, and it was difficult to keep them silent, especially the younger children. We got them all into the forest a good distance away from the camp and told them to wait for our return. After taking a drink of water from our skins, we gave the captives all our food and water to share around. It wouldn't be enough to sate their hunger or slake their thirst, as there were so many of them, but we promised to provide them with all we could when we returned.

The three of us crept back to the camp and surveyed it from the tree line. It was obvious we would be heavily outnumbered. Gweilt and Liam both looked to me for a plan.

"I will go in alone, and stand in the middle of the camp," I said. "When I am in position, both of you start setting the outer tents on fire with arrows. Once all of the outer tents have taken light, one of you come to me and the other stay here to pick off any runners. Gweilt, you are the better archer, so you stay here. Not one of them leaves this place."

Gweilt nodded and said, "Not one."

The battle was short, chaotic, and vicious. My training served me well. Between myself and Liam, sixty enemies were dead within minutes. Another twenty were caught by Gweilt's arrows as they tried to flee. When nothing in the camp stirred, we piled up the bodies, tents, and the cage, and set the whole thing on fire. I watched the flames as they consumed the entire pile of filth in an elegant, violent conflagration. Visions of my brave and beautiful wife burning to death in our home flashed through my mind. Images of my sweet daughter's tiny broken form passed across my eyes. This wasn't enough. Not nearly enough.

We arrived back at the homestead a day later, and they were overjoyed to see their children and young women. Most of the captives had come from other places. The homesteaders promised to see them all home safely. The old man gave my daughter back to me, cleaned and wrapped lovingly in a swath of soft fabric with fresh-cut herbs and flowers. I thanked him, and we set off back home.

Gweilt and Liam helped me dig a grave for my daughter right beside my wife under the willow tree. We buried her there next to her mother, and in addition to another large, smooth stone, I left the little wooden chicken with its hodgepodge of feathers attached. I thanked Liam and Gweilt and hugged them. They left to return to their own families.

I sat down at the foot of the graves and mourned. I had one purpose while they were alive: to keep them safe. I had failed them. Now I had two purposes: to hunt down and eliminate this evil wherever it might surface, and to reunite with my family.

I sat in contemplation at their graves until long after the sun had set.

# Chapter Twenty-Two

I woke up in my apartment with tears on my face.

I sat up in the bed and looked at the raven, still perched on the footboard. He had his head bowed, though his eyes were open. I decided not to speak until I was fully awake. I went to the restroom and washed my face. I set out a dish of fresh, cool water and the reheated remains of a meal for the raven. I made a cup of coffee. I...realized I was putting off the inevitable and made myself return to the bedroom.

"Would you care to join me for breakfast?" I asked the raven.

He slowly raised his head and looked at me. "I would be honored," he said softly. He spread his wings to fly, so I turned around to get out of his way. I heard a few heavy flaps as he took wing, and before I could move I felt a gentle weight settle on my left shoulder.

*Is this really happening?*

"Yes," replied the raven, though I hadn't spoken. "It is hard, but I am afraid it is the truth."

I nodded, accepting this. I had no reason to doubt the raven's sincerity. I collected the food, water, and coffee from the small kitchen and sat down at my dining table. The raven hopped off my shoulder onto the tabletop, took a drink of the water, and dug into the food. I let him eat as I went over my memories of the past several months.

My journey had started under the guidance of Huginn, who was associated with thought. Over months, it was true that I had changed the way I thought enough to shift my perspective and pull myself out of unemployment and homelessness. I had also seen the truth about the group I was hanging out with and had gone home to reunite with my family.

Recently I had been under the guidance of Muninn, who was associated with memory, and it had only been over the past week or so that I had lived through what seemed like *millennia* of bad memories. Some of them were among the most horrific events I could imagine.

Muninn was looking at me, his eating apparently finished. "Some of them were good," he said.

I looked at him, sipping my coffee, waiting for an explanation. He continued, "It is important – critically important – that you remember the good parts as much as the bad. You got to see some good friends, many of whom you have not yet met in this lifetime, as well as the wife and daughter you lost. You got to spend some time with them, got to know the content of their character. You got to meet the Allfather face to face. You gained insight and understanding of your own motivations."

He paused for a moment at this. "At least, you gained some insight. Understanding will come in time. But only if you remember the good you experienced. A litany of horrors without balance does you no good. Remember that this seeking is about addressing the toll your chosen path has taken on you." He spoke again, and I gasped when Odin's voice came out, "Please do not let the darkness overtake you."

I stared at him. "The Darkness...."

Muninn didn't miss the emphasis I placed on the second word. "The same," he said, confirming my unspoken question. "You have encountered it several times during this lifetime, though not so directly as you did months ago in that park...or last night."

"Those shadowy figures in the valley?" I asked. Muninn nodded.

"I don't understand," I said. "Haven't I always resisted the Darkness?"

"You have," Muninn answered. "Though your resistance has become a sort of...gateway...over the course of your many lifetimes." At my questioning look he continued. "You see," he said, "the only way to avoid evil's lure, aside from just avoiding evil altogether – which is not possible – is to devote yourself entirely to a good purpose. Even then, when you confront evil, when you touch it, it touches you back. It leaves a...stain."

I raised my eyebrows. "I'm stained?"

"Yes," replied Muninn. "In a way. You felt it during your training, did you not?"

I vividly remembered the sickly tingle as I had battled the shadowy figures. I nodded.

"There are many reasons why the Allfather shed a tear for you that night," Muninn said, "but only one reason he gave you the warning he did about the Darkness overtaking you. Do you know why he gave you that warning?"

I didn't have to think about it long. "My motives," I said.

Muninn nodded. "You were seeking vengeance when you asked for the mantle," he said. I started to retort but he cut me off. "Nobody denies you had a right to pursue and punish those foul creatures that took your wife and daughter from you. Still, vengeance is a short-term motivation. At least, it is supposed to be. You, however, have trouble letting things go. You took this event personally...*too* personally. You have carried the heavy burden of that mantle for thousands of years. It has taken a heavy toll on you."

"You mean that it was never meant to be carried by a mortal?" I asked.

"To the contrary," he said, "that particular mantle can *only* be carried by a mortal. That said, the price of carrying it is high. Say instead that it was meant to be carried by a *different* mortal each generation, to spread out its precious toll across many. You – you alone – have carried it for *hundreds* of lifetimes despite the cost. It has stained you in ways that you cannot yet fathom. More accurately, the evil you have chosen to face has stained you. The mantle is just power."

I thought about that for a few moments, sipping coffee.

"It has changed how I see the world," I said.

"And people," said Muninn. "And life."

"Care to explain that?" I asked.

Muninn thought for a moment before answering. "We will start with people," he said. "You have faced so much darkness that it has tainted your opinion of people. You are always suspicious of them and their motives. You have actually gotten very good at guessing motives, and the actions people will take to achieve their goals. It provides you a measure of advantage when battling against the forces of darkness. Especially if you get close enough to touch them, in which case you can identify the evil within them and learn everything you need to know about them from a handshake and a look in their eyes."

"How is that a problem?" I asked. I had never considered my instincts about people to be a stain.

"You do it to *everyone*," Muninn said. "Without exception, you judge all people according to their motives."

"Oh."

"The real problem is that *all* adults have motives, and they're not always 'good'...but that does not mean they are 'evil,'" said Muninn. "Specifically, they are not the kind of evil the mantle was meant to address. Consider a woman protecting her marriage. She may be considering some pretty nefarious notions when you meet her. Instead of considering the larger picture, you only see nefarious motives and judge accordingly."

"Oh," I said again. "That's bad."

Muninn stared at me and said, quite deadpan, "You are the king of understatement."

I laughed as he took a drink of water. He shut me up by saying, "It is only funny because you have not actually taken any action against an innocent. Consider what could have happened if another person with the mantle and your current problem in this regard had assessed you in the same way just before you asked for the mantle."

That killed my laughter instantly. "Oh," I said again. "I see." I took another sip of coffee in an attempt to cover my discomfort. "What about life?" I asked.

"Life has become, for you, a *cause*," said Muninn. "Not a natural progression of good and bad moments, but a *mission*."

"A mission?" I asked. "I'm not in special op...."

"This is not a joke," Muninn snapped quietly. "All power has a purpose. The mantle has a very specific purpose, and as I have told you, it is power. The mantle is meant to pass to different mortals each generation because it has a tendency to take over. The mantle has taken sway over your life...it has almost taken over your free will."

That was enough to put me back in my place. I shut my mouth properly and listened.

"Think of the mantle as a torch, or a flashlight," Muninn said. "It provides insight about your path, so you are much more effective in walking. The flashlight does not function without its component parts, however. It is a framework, but it still requires a bulb and batteries, as well as a hand to guide it." He paused, presumably to make sure he chose the correct words. "If the mantle is the framework of the flashlight, then the bulb is conscious thought and the batteries are experience."

I nodded, understanding.

"The guiding hand is free will," he finished.

My jaw dropped. "Uhh..." I began, and finished with, "uh-oh."

"Now you begin to see the scope of the problem," Muninn said. "The mantle may only act on what it can see. Your will guides it and your mind assesses what it illuminates. Your experience informs your actions, not just *how* to act, but *whether or not you should*. Can you see what would happen if that power were able to guide itself?"

"Not one human being would survive that," I said.

Muninn considered this a moment and said, "Perhaps in the end, but not by your hand." At my questioning glance he continued, "The mantle and the experience you have make you powerful. You are cold death with just about anything that comes to hand, including your hands. You are powerful, but you are still mortal. I would think that you would have understood this from your experiences over the past week. In any case, the mantle itself could be put at grave risk. It must be carried by a mortal, and it may not harm an innocent. Those are the two laws that govern its existence. Without conscious thought and experience, free will cannot act in an informed and responsible manner. In this circumstance, the mantle may violate one or both laws and cease to exist. If this occurs, nothing would stand in the way of this insidious evil, and it could take firm root and grow unchecked, leading eventually to the downfall of mankind."

"That's...really bad," I said.

"Again, king of understatement," he said. "The mantles were created to give mankind a kind of equity with the forces of darkness that threaten them. They work together to provide a helping hand, to give humanity a fighting chance against those forces that would keep them from transcending their condition."

"There's more than one mantle?" I asked.

"There are *thousands*, young one," he said. "Evil has many faces, many names, and many manifestations. It is truly an insidious enemy. The mantle you bear was designed to protect children in specific circumstances. It was created to free them from the grasp of an evil that seeks to either twist them into a form useful to it or kill them. It is *not* a universal cure."

"May I ask you to clarify something?" I asked. Muninn nodded. "What do you mean by 'twist them into a form useful to it'?"

"This will be difficult for you to grasp," he answered. "You must think of it in terms of mortal time...in terms of mortal generations." He paced around the bowl of water, looking down into it. "When you first took on the mantle to pursue your wife and daughter's murderers, did you know the identity of the enemy?"

"No," I replied. "Some raiders. They had taken some livestock and grain, and...."

"Mere raiders do not take children," he said, cutting me off. "Those men were taking children to twist them to their purposes. They intended to build a nation of like individuals."

My jaw dropped again, but I managed to whisper out, "A *nation*? I wiped out a *nation*?"

Muninn looked up to me with more of a serious expression than I would have thought possible. "The seminal members were there, yes. Their intent was to either abuse the males until they capitulated or use them as slave labor. The females were to be raised and indoctrinated as," his voice turned bitter and growly, "...breeding stock. Those who gave them too much resistance at the beginning of their captivity were sacrificed as an example to the others."

"My daughter..." I began.

"Was killed because she was strong, and brave, and had a wonderful father who taught her the value of life and self-worth," said Muninn. "You loved her very well, and it served her better than you know. Her Papa was her hero, and she did all she could to help the other children you found. Many of them went on to raise strong, healthy, happy children of their own. They all taught their children the lessons they learned during that ordeal, and their children did the same, and so on. That sweet little girl's courage of a day and night saved thousands of lives."

I couldn't help the tears that sprang to my eyes, part mourning and part fierce pride. "She was precious," I said.

"She still is," Muninn said. "Her words and actions still save lives. But only because you used the mantle responsibly, the way it was meant to be used. Because you saved the other children, who were able to pass on her legacy through the generations."

"Where did they go?" I asked. I wasn't sure what specifically I wanted to hear, but I knew they both deserved a good afterlife.

The raven approximated a sigh. "On," he said. At my morose look he said, "I know it is not the answer you want, but it is the best answer I can give you. I can provide you with a few vague details of their existences, but not a complete accounting. Their paths are their own."

"Are they together? Are they happy?"

"Sometimes," Muninn said, "and sometimes." He paused a moment and continued with a question. "What have you experienced over the past week?"

I thought about it and answered, "Some of my past lives."

"Where?" asked Muninn.

I thought about it some more. "Finland, Scotland, Ireland, America – I think – and some other places," I said. I started to get it and felt a little dumb. "Oh. When I ask where they went there's not a simple answer. I meant...."

"Did they go to the good place or the bad place?" Muninn finished for me. He let me think for a few moments before continuing. "I told you during this seeking that Heaven and Hell are what you make them. What do you think I meant by that?"

"I'm...honestly not sure," I replied.

Muninn looked at me, and it seemed a bit...hard. Flat. Maybe a little – just a tiny bit – amused? "Where did *you* go?" he asked.

"What?" Don't judge me. This is way harder than I make it seem. Plus, Rina said I couldn't get answers without asking questions.

Okay, it was a little pathetic.

"You bring a new definition to the term 'dense,'" Muninn said. I balked a little at that but held my silence. Barely. Muninn must have taken pity on me, because he approximated another sigh and began to explain it for me.

"You have experienced portions of several lifetimes over the past week," he said. "Each of those lifetimes is separated from the previous and next one by three things...three events, if you will: a death, a transition, and a birth. Your question refers specifically to the transition. You die, you go somewhere for a while, and then you are born again to repeat the cycle. Where did *you* go during your transitions?"

I just sat there for a minute, silent. I hadn't really considered it like that before. "Wait...we just *visit* the eternal realms of bliss and punishment?" I asked incredulously.

"Some do," confirmed Muninn. "Some stay. It depends on the person and what they believe they need or deserve. The length of the transition period also depends upon the person."

"Care to explain?" I asked.

"What is the difference between the Christian Hell, the Jewish Gehenna, and the Nordic Niflheim?" he asked me.

"Umm...," I responded, "one is really icy, and the other two are fiery?" Muninn actually cackled. I thought it was clever. I tried again. "Duration?"

"Duration," he confirmed. "Hell is portrayed as permanent, Gehenna is more like a visit to the cosmic principal's office where sinners get impurities burned off before moving on to Heaven, and Niflheim is an icy realm where oathbreakers, murderers, and adulterers are pursued, tormented, and devoured by frost giants."

I laughed heartily. Muninn cocked his head to one side. "Sorry," I laughed out. "I just got that joke." Muninn cocked his head the other direction. "Oh, come on," I said, "that's hilarious. The Old Norse notion of eternal punishment was to get chased through the snow, torn apart by Dr. Cold Hands, and wind up as an icy cold shite in a frozen wasteland." I howled with renewed laughter. Muninn joined me.

When our laughter had subsided – and that took a while – Muninn looked at me and said, "You see the point, at least."

"I think so," I said. "Hell, or eternal punishment, tends to resemble the worst parts of everyday life. For those in the hotter parts of the world, Hell is endless, intense heat. For those in cold landscapes, like the Norse, it's endless ice storms. No shelter from the elements seems a constant. The only thing that really seems to vary, though, is the duration of the punishment."

"And Heaven?" asked Muninn.

"There doesn't seem to be any consistent description of it beyond 'your best ever happy place,'" I said. "Eternal life. Peace. Tranquility. No suffering. Overall, though, it seems to be very subjective."

"It is," said Muninn. "The same types of cultural correlations exist. Those in hot, desert areas tend to see it as a tropical place, a lush garden of some sort. Those in the northern reaches tend to see it as shelter from the cold, a comfortable hall with fires, food, drink, and family. Some go to a little place of their own in various places in the land of the Fae. Some create their own demesne – what you aptly called their 'best ever happy place.' One thing I think you will find common among them is family."

"Family?" I asked. "Really?"

Muninn nodded. "Religions are frameworks," he said. "They provide you with notions of good and bad afterlives and give you some rules to follow as you live out your life. If you follow the rules you get to go to the good place. If not, you are condemned to the bad place. Do you know what all religions share?"

"Family," I said.

Muninn nodded again. "There is almost always a direct tie to family lineage." He paced over to the little bowl of water and took a drink. I sipped my coffee. "The so-called 'big three' – Christianity, Judaism, and Islam – all trace their origins back to three descendants of Abraham. The Nordic path leads back to three brothers: Odin, Vili and Ve. They go back even farther to the first humans Adam and Eve, or to Askr and Embla in the Norse path."

"I hadn't thought of that before," I said. "Seems like a pretty big coincidence."

"I would think that you know better by now," said Muninn.

"I know," I said. "What seems like coincidence is most often a synchronicity instead." I thought for a moment. "When I spoke with Tim, he gave me the impression that, uh, the Nordic gods are just ancestors...not gods."

"You do understand that the term 'gods' is subjective, and just means 'advanced beings,' do you not?" Muninn asked.

"Well, yes and no," I responded honestly.

"That is because you humans vastly overuse the word," he said. "You use it interchangeably with the word 'master.'"

I chuckled and said, "You mean how people refer to themselves as the 'god' of something they're good at."

"Yes," Muninn said, perhaps a little bitterly. "In a way, this comes from the bards and skalds who embellished the original stories to get better food. When the stories were written down, the labels stuck. The Church was all too happy with these labels, as they were provided with an easily refuted and controlled opposition."

That rang a bell, and not a comfortable one. "Controlled opposition...."

"Yes," Muninn continued, "controlled opposition. An imaginary or faceless adversary to struggle against gives humans a unifying rallying point to seek victory over. The same was done to many other cultural groups, not just the Norse."

"For what purpose?" I asked.

Muninn sighed and said, "Humans are humans. People are people. Name a purpose, and controlled opposition can be used to get people moving in the right direction to achieve it. The most common application has been conquest. Create an enemy in a rival nation, and the people in your nation will do their best to conquer it."

"Wow," I said. "A lot of death and destruction then, huh?"

"Do not mistake me," Muninn said. "Controlled opposition can be quite useful in the right circumstance."

"Such as?"

"The Ten Commandments are a good example," he responded.

I started to ask a question but closed my mouth and opened my ears instead. Muninn nodded in a measure of respect. Apparently, I was learning to shut my big mouth and think before speaking, and that was a good thing.

"The Commandments themselves are not the opposition," he said. "They are the Law, the desired objective. The opposition is the one you call Satan. Aptly, this title means 'accuser.' His given name is

Helel, more commonly translated through Latin as Lucifer. His tool for conquest of the individual is called 'sin,' which is the result of breaking the Law. Do you follow?"

"Yes," I replied.

"Something not many people realize about the Commandments: the first five deal with how you are expected to treat God, and the last five deal with how you are expected to treat other humans," he said. "So, the objective becomes a little clearer. First, if you're going to follow God, don't hold any other gods...because there is only one source of truth. Second, no idols – a carved image will not do anything but waste your time and give you a false impression of something that is incomprehensible in physical form. Third, names have power, so it is very important to use them properly. Fourth, take a day each week for worship and reflection. Fifth, honor your father and mother, who made you and teach you to be a good person. Still following?"

I nodded.

"Very well," said Muninn. "We move on to how you are expected to treat other humans. No murdering, no adultery, no theft, no false testimony, and no coveting." He looked at me and asked, "Did you catch it?"

"Catch what?"

"Why are they in the same list? Why not call Lucifer by his proper name instead of 'devil' or 'Satan?'" He continued looking at me, apparently waiting for me to catch up. I didn't.

"I don't understand," I said.

"When you last spoke with Tim, what did you realize?" he asked.

I thought about it. "You're referring to the notion that humans are...semi-divine," I said. "The idea that all humans have a little piece of the Creator within them."

Muninn nodded and waited for me to continue my line of thought. "By that logic, I can see what you're getting at. If humans are actually part of the Creator, it would make sense that the Law would include both how to treat the Creator and how to treat other humans, since they share attributes."

"Yes," said Muninn. His little black eyes were glittering. It was a little creepy.

"I only have one problem with that line of thought," I said.

Muninn sighed, ruffling his feathers. "You want evidence," he said.

"Well, yes," I said. "You must admit this is a pretty big leap to take."

"Only if you are uninformed," he responded. "Why the promise of Heaven and the threat of Hell?"

I had to think about this a little. It was obvious from the wording of his question that he was referring to the old "carrot and stick" metaphor. "Power has a tendency to corrupt," I said. "Our experiences tend to color our perspective, so a heavy incentive to act right would seem reasonable. Of course, it's also reasonable to believe that the Law is the Law, and there are consequences for breaking laws."

Muninn didn't give up. "Have you read the gospel?" he asked. "Specifically, what did Yeshua tell the people he healed?"

"I haven't read it yet," I said. "You may have noticed I've been a bit busy recently." I smiled at Muninn but he didn't return anything similarly jovial. I sipped my coffee.

"I will enlighten you, then," he said, "though you should take the initiative to read it for yourself." He spread his wings a bit, and then recomposed himself. "After almost every healing, he tells the person, 'your faith has made you well.'"

That startled me a little. "Wait," I said. "That doesn't make any sense!"

"On the contrary," he said, "it makes perfect sense...if they healed themselves."

I thought he looked a little smug, but I checked myself and realized I was just experiencing some good old-fashioned cognitive dissonance. The "official" story was that a man named Jesus – his real name was Yeshua – had shown up in the middle of some hard times, healed a bunch of people, preached about salvation, and been killed through the grueling process of crucifixion. The story said he was the Son of God, the Savior of human beings.

What Muninn was saying, and Tim had said as well, was that we were all children of God, and all had a tiny piece of the Creator inside us. People were still arguing, more than two thousand years after the story had concluded, about the divinity of Christ. If Muninn and Tim were correct, then Yeshua did have a divine nature, because we *all* did. And if that was true...then it all *did* make sense. A distinctly uncomfortable amount of sense.

"You begin to see the truth," Muninn said.

If this was true, then....

"You're saying that Yeshua was what?" I asked. "*Better at being human* than the rest of us?"

"That is a nice, simple way of putting it," he said. "Humans have *power*, but they generally do not recognize it."

My brain was starting to hurt. He was saying that Yeshua was human, all the way human, and that we *all* had the same power – at least over ourselves – as Yeshua had. Could that really be true?

Muninn took another drink of water as I watched him. If it was true, it sure put a whole new spin on the Bible: Old Testament, history book, New Testament, instruction manual. Wow. Just...wow.

If it was true....

"Please do not strain yourself," Muninn said. I gave him a withering glance, and he cackled again. "If there is one thing that never gets old, comedically speaking, it is watching people try to think their way through a quandary. The facial expressions alone are priceless."

I sighed, feeling even more like a monkey making love to a football. "Thank you?" I said, adding the question mark because technically his comment could be taken as a compliment, but it was doubtful.

"I was speaking honestly," said Muninn. "There is no need for you to puzzle this out just now. It is a matter of faith. Say, for now, that Yeshua meant to be a good example – the perfect example – for humanity to strive toward."

"I can accept that," I said. "My only question about that is...."

"Whether he was truly the son of the Creator?" Muninn finished for me. I nodded. "I would think the answer to that question is obviously yes. The story of Yeshua is very straightforward. It is even backed up by the prophets from the Old Testament." He considered for a moment, then said, "I have never understood the position of the Satanists, myself. That book only has one ending, and it is quite clear the Darkness is defeated. Why would one voluntarily throw in on the losing side of a fight with those kinds of stakes on the line?" He shook his head, presumably to clear it. "Humans are truly strange creatures sometimes. In any case...."

"You were explaining the concept of controlled opposition?" I asked.

"Ah, yes," Muninn said. "The devil. Satan. Lucifer. The Adversary." He paced back and forth on the table, head down, seemingly thinking. After a few moments, he looked down at the water in his drinking bowl and cocked his head to one side. "Tell me about Lucifer," he said quietly.

"I don't know much," I admitted. "Just the standard story everybody knows. Lucifer was one of the higher orders of angels, and when God created humans and declared them the proverbial apple of His eye, Lucifer got jealous and declared war, then got thrown into the pit."

Muninn nodded, still not looking at me, and asked, "What is the origin of that story? Where does it come from?"

I had no answer for that. I presumed that it came from the Bible, but I couldn't remember specifically where. I looked a question at Muninn and shook my head.

Muninn was slowly shaking his head in return.

"It's not...in the Bible?" I asked.

Muninn was still slowly shaking his head.

"But that's Church doctrine!" I said, admittedly with more gusto than I intended. "We've all been raised to believe there's a devil and a place of eternal punishment called Hell!"

"True," said Muninn. "There is an adversary, and there is a place of punishment."

Wait, what? How can it exist if it doesn't exist?

He answered my unspoken question. "There are several references to a 'devil' and 'Satan' in both the Old and New Testaments, though there is only a single reference – in the book of Isaiah – to 'Lucifer,' or rather to the 'morning star,' which has generally been removed and replaced with 'Day Star' and 'son of dawn,'" he said. "There are also several references to Sheol, Gehenna, and hell, though the most frequent descriptions refer to the 'lake of fire,' a 'blazing furnace,' and the 'realm of the dead.'"

"But then...." I started.

Muninn cut me off. "There is also a doctrine that states what humans hold true on Earth will be upheld in Heaven." He looked at me with one little black eye, as though waiting for me to get it.

I had to disappoint him again. I just wasn't getting it. I wasn't understanding, and it drove me a little crazy. I had been looking for this my whole life – and perhaps for many whole lifetimes – and now that it was being laid out before me, I couldn't grasp it. Muninn seemed to pick up on how lost I was and settled himself directly in front of me. I met his gaze and sighed out a heavy breath.

My eyes welled with angry and disappointed tears. Had all this – the danger, the heartbreak, the estrangement from my family, the loss of some friends, the loneliness, the trauma of living through all those horrors of the past week – been for nothing?

"No," Muninn said quietly. "The search for truth is never fruitless. It can be hard, cold, lonely, and costly...but it is never done in vain. You have paid a terrible price for this knowledge, and I am afraid you will continue to pay that price for many years to come. You have earned this knowledge. You only need to see it." He paused, only for a moment, then said, "Your previously learned assumptions are blocking your perception. Sweep them aside, replace them with what you have recently learned, and look again. Ask the right question. *See.*"

*The right question*...and then I had it.

*How do all the religions fit together so that everyone can be saved and not suffer eternal punishment?*

Pieces of the vast puzzle started slamming together in my mind. It hurt. A lot. I think I screamed.

We humans were created as immortal souls. Not bodies with souls, but souls with bodies.

Each of us had a piece of the Creator within us, as per the act of creation. In the same way that mortal parents each contribute components to the creation of a baby, the Creator had given of Himself to create humans.

Reincarnation was real, and lives were separated by three events: death, transition, and birth. The Christian notion of being "born again" suddenly took on a whole new meaning.

The transition could be a period of bliss, punishment, or reflection, depending on the individual's personal beliefs, actions, and resulting expectations. Some stayed in their transition permanently, or at least long-term. Considering that the notion of punishment tended to be commensurate with one's sins, it didn't make sense that punishment could be truly permanent. *Forever* was a long, long time, after all. Spending an eternity in the throes of all-out torture for stealing five bucks from your dad to eat lunch at school once seems a bit extreme.

The concepts of the devil and hell seemed to be, at least in part, a nefarious boogeyman story, but with real backing and a really good reason. If we were entrusted with a small spark of the Creator, well...even a tiny spark of infinity, by its very definition, would represent *infinite power*. That power was intended for good, for creation. Using it for anything else would represent a serious threat. A *really* serious threat. To everyone and everything. The threat didn't have to be a nuclear bomb, where everything would just suddenly be over with a giant boom. It would most likely be something far more insidious and effective. Something far less visible and less impactful to the greater whole. Something like twisting our children to achieve the objective slowly over time.

I gasped with the weight of the realization.

*Free will*. Of all creation, humans had the ability to *choose*. Evil, which I had come to know as the Darkness, was not only real, but was also the most insane, nefarious, horrible thing I had ever imagined. Free will was not only a gift, it was a massive responsibility. One that most adults misused on a frequent basis with casual abandon. The one group that couldn't discern proper choice very well? The only group that didn't have much experience: *children*.

There was an Adversary, as surely as there was a Creator. It was *us*. Specifically, our free will. It was just as easy to choose the wrong thing as it was to choose the right thing; many times, it was easier to choose the wrong thing. In a way, the entire human race was an ongoing grand experiment right from the beginning. We were entrusted with power, and there was only one reliable, definitive way to see if we were worthy of that power: to be judged by our choices. How we chose to use the power we were entrusted with would determine our worthiness to possess it. Our own choices would determine our destination...because we would create it.

I was seeking salvation, but the only one guilty of condemning me...was me. My own choices. I wasn't a monster, but all the things I felt bad about were the result of my own free will. Sure, according to some religions, I could simply ask forgiveness, repent, and live to rectify my poor choices or at least make better ones. I might even get to go to the good place. To me, though, this didn't seem like...*enough*. Long and hard experience had taught me that power doesn't just pass from hand to hand without consequences. According to what I had seen over the past week, I had asked for even more power than I already had – the mantle – to address a personal injustice. I was told very directly that the cost of taking on that mantle would be high, and I had asked for it anyway.

I alone had made the choice to accept that mantle, and it had cost me dearly. I had also made the choice to retain the mantle for apparently *thousands* of years. The consuming obsession with bringing back my wife and daughter while carrying the mantle had driven me to the brink of insanity in at least one lifetime. What had it done to me over the centuries?

I had to set aside those thoughts and focus on what I was really seeking: the truth about the divine. According to what I had learned over the past couple of years since I began seeking, the divine lived in all of us, and likely, all around us. The conceptual notion of the Christian God was that this entity was omniscient, omnipresent, and omnipotent – all-knowing, everywhere at all times, and all-powerful. Logically, the only way to be everywhere all the time was to *be* everywhere. To be all-knowing and all-powerful was to be the *source* of all knowledge and power. Yet another small but poignant piece of evidence was that we were all literally children of God, possessing some small measure of divinity God had imparted to us upon creation.

The whole thing started to make a little more sense. If God had given us this little piece of divinity, it would make good sense to protect it in the event free will was misused to harm it: no murdering, no stealing, no lying, no adultery, no coveting. In other words, we had all been given the gift of power...and we were each personally responsible for how we used it.

The Law – also known as the Ten Commandments – were not just a list of rules to follow, though. They were a recipe for a peaceful and good civilization where everyone had power. The perfect civilization that we all dream of was possible. However, removing even one of the Commandments would cause that utopia to collapse. We – the Wandering – were looking for a place where we could live peacefully with one another, and it was right in front of us the whole time...if we simply had the *will* to create and live it.

Wow. Just wow. The hardest part of having the kind of power that free will imparts? Realizing that having power is not the same as having all the answers. Realizing that despite having power, you need help. I mean, we don't put a sword or gun in the hands of a toddler because we know they could seriously harm – even kill – others, or themselves. Yet we had been handed a loaded bazooka...by our ancestors who had taken the knowledge of good and evil from the garden of Eden, and – *please help me* – had become "like God." I remembered that part from Genesis with great trepidation.

So, what did all this mean for me and the rest of the Wandering?

That we did not have to choose between religions and gamble our immortal souls. As long as we sought the truth and kept our free will in check, asking for help when we needed it and striving to live up to the good example Yeshua had provided us, we would be just fine. Our ancestry was important, and their experiences could serve as useful examples as we sought the right spiritual path. After all, as mortals, we had to be able to relate our life experience to our spiritual path. Studying the way our ancestors lived was a good way to do that. Not only our distant ancestors, but our recent ones, too: our parents, aunts and uncles, grandparents, great-grandparents, and so on.

I had a lot to think about.

# Chapter
# Twenty-Three

I looked up when I heard a sharp, strange tapping on my door. I looked at Muninn with knit eyebrows. He sighed and ducked his head, his feathers ruffling. "I was hoping he would not show up, as he irritates me to no end." At my continued questioning glance, he said, "That is my brother."

I walked to the door and pulled it open slowly. The first raven, Huginn, was standing in front of the door. "Poe much?" I asked him. He did his little foot-to-foot happy dance, laughing.

That's when I saw that he wasn't alone. Two men stepped in front of the doorway, and I stood in shock. One was Tim, dressed in jeans and work boots and a tight white t-shirt. The other was...well, it was obviously the old man from the park, but he was dressed very differently. He now wore dark slacks and button-down shirt and tie, with polished black dress shoes, a black leather eye patch, a black fedora, and a fashionable gray traveling cloak.

I didn't know what to say, so I just stood there gaping. Go ahead. Laugh. I'd like to know what you'd say if they showed up at your door. There's a *huge* difference between *thinking* you know and *knowing* firsthand. A huge difference. I'm actually surprised I didn't faint. So, I gathered my voice the best I could and said, "Please, be welcome to my hall...all three of you."

The two men smiled and bowed their heads to me before stepping over the threshold into my humble little apartment. They both shook my offered hand as they entered, the old man removing his hat. I gestured to my table, where Muninn still sat, and offered them a seat. I walked to the kitchen and found three glasses before I realized I didn't have any good drink.

I felt a gentle hand on my shoulder and turned my head to find the old man by my side. His thin, hawkish face, framed by a generous shoulder-length waterfall of iron-gray hair, smiled mildly. He said softly, "Please do not trouble yourself, son. This time *I* brought the refreshments. Come sit down with us and share our company."

I nodded and let him steer me back to the table. I sat.

The old man sat down across from me and beside Tim. They were all looking at me. I felt like I was in trouble and, ashamed, hung my head.

"You have just swallowed a very bitter pill, son," said the old man. "Most cannot take it and will do just about anything they can to protect the status quo of their chosen belief system. Knowing that you might be wrong, or at least do not have all the answers, is difficult. Men and women have lost their minds over less."

I didn't look up. "I feel as though I have failed," I said. "Not just myself, but others."

A pregnant silence hung in the air for a few moments before the old man said, "Failed? You have far exceeded our expectations, in every way."

I did look up at him at this unexpected statement. "Yeah?" I asked warily.

Tim spoke now. "Absolutely," he said. "Why did you think we were here?"

Confused and flustered, I answered, "To...take me out." After another awkward pause, they laughed. All of them. Hard. I kept my silence.

Tim said, "You thought we were here to *kill* you?" They all laughed some more. I took it in stride.

"There is only one thing about your actions that disappoints me," said the old man. Everybody fell silent, though it was obvious they were all barely concealing smiles and chuckles. "You thought we were here to kill you," he continued, "...and you *let us in?*" Everybody lost it again, laughing out loud. I joined in with some chuckles of my own, pinching the bridge of my nose and shaking my head. "Despite that, your instincts seem to be functioning properly. We are not here to harm you. We are here to thank you and help you if we can."

"Thank me...?" I couldn't imagine why they would be thanking me.

"That mantle is a heavy burden," the old man said. "It can do a lot of good, in the right hands, but it exacts a heavy toll on the one that carries it. Most who have carried it have given it up after a single use. You have held onto it for a long, long time. I told you when you first asked for it that the mantle was purposed for another, and that the cost could be dangerously high. You took that burden upon yourself anyway, and your use of it has saved lives. Too many to enumerate now, but when I last knew the number it was in the tens of thousands."

"Really?" I asked.

"Really," he answered. "Directly, you have saved thousands of children."

I'm not a math whiz, but even I noticed that discrepancy. "Actions always have consequences," he said, apparently picking up on my unspoken question. "You saved a bunch of young people directly, but the consequences of each life saved are far-reaching.

Parents, siblings, other family members, friends and neighbors, future generations...every life is connected, in some way, to a multitude of others. So, for every life you saved directly, you saved or positively altered a number of others." His eyes met mine and he said slowly, "Tens of thousands."

I thought about that and nodded. It felt good to know that I had helped others.

"The cost, to you, has become too high for our liking," the old man said. "You have done a truly immeasurable amount of good and have carried the mantle admirably...but the things you have needed to do, over time, have begun to twist you." He paused a moment, then said, "We do not enjoy watching you suffer in this way. We would like you to give up the mantle."

I sighed heavily and hung my head.

"We cannot take it from you," he said. "This is not a punishment. You must understand that. We want to bring you some measure of relief, so you may finally *live*, for yourself, rather than serving your fellow mortals in a state of perpetual loneliness and agony. It is tearing you apart, and you deserve better than that."

I understood what he was saying. I had felt that deep well of loneliness and despair inside me since I was a young child. So many betrayals of my trust and love and friendship had led me to view other people as liars and cruel wildcards that were always looking for the best way to use and discard me, even after I had known them for years and despite what I did to earn their loyalty. The most recent example – the group and band I had been part of – was an extreme and poignant one. I had left my *family* to pursue what I was convinced was the "right" path, and despite my loyalty and friendship I had been unceremoniously thrown out on my ass. I was perfectly okay with that result, given the circumstances, but it didn't excuse the massive cost I had incurred.

"May I ask a few questions?" I asked.

"I think more than a few answers would be perfectly reasonable, given your service," said the old man.

"I never got your name," I said to him.

He smiled and met my eyes. "I have many of those," he said. "You would know me as...."

"...Odin," I breathed.

He bowed his head in a little nod to me, his eyes never leaving mine. "I am most pleased to make your acquaintance," he said.

I looked at Tim and asked, "Your name isn't Tim, is it?"

He shook his head slowly, with a small smile. "My name is Thor," he said.

My heart was hammering in my chest. I looked at the two ravens on the table, who were both doing their best impressions of innocent bystanders. I already knew their names: Huginn and Muninn. I looked back to Odin, trying to keep my world from shifting out from under me.

There is a *huge* difference between thinking you know and knowing for certain.

A *huge* difference.

I'm not sure how long I sat there, silent, trying not to simply pass out.

Eventually I managed to croak out, "What must I do?"

They were all looking at me. I could feel the weight of their gazes on me like a heavy blanket. It was all I could do to not glare back at them all with naked belligerence. I closed my eyes and took a series of deep breaths, one after another, forcing myself to calm down.

"That," came Odin's deep and quiet voice, "is a perfect example of why we are asking you to relinquish the mantle."

I opened my eyes to see Odin handling and examining a bottle of mead. I raised an eyebrow in question.

"That rage you just experienced was not your own," he answered.

I rocked back as if I'd been slapped. "What?" I asked incredulously.

"Make no mistake," he said. "You have quite enough enmity within yourself, most of it with very good reason. You have felt like a pawn most of your life, less some*one* than some*thing*, to be toyed with, used, and discarded by those you value. However, weary of dealing with that constant struggle, you gave up some of your control of it to the mantle. The mantle, which has no power to make conscious decisions, now has a measure of control over when and how to act. It uses your own rage and despair as fuel. The rage you just felt at having your paradigm challenged, while it was reasonable to assume it was yours, was actually the mantle classifying us as a threat and preparing to act...through you." He paused for a few moments, uncorking the bottle and turning his gaze back to me. "Do you see the problem this situation presents?"

I just sat there, stunned. How could I not have seen this before? I wasn't misusing the mantle. *It was using me*. I suddenly understood why Odin had brought Thor along. That wasn't a fight I could win. I shivered. I gathered myself a little more and said, "Yes. I see now."

Odin nodded, and I thought I saw a small measure of respect cross his features. I looked at Thor, and he nodded at me too. When I looked back to Odin, he was pouring the bottle of mead into a large, ornately-carved drinking horn. I had no idea where it had come from, or the bottle of mead, since neither of them were carrying any bags and neither one of those things were something you could hide in a pocket. I glanced back to Thor and he smiled and gave me a shrug. I turned my gaze back to Odin and decided not to ask.

"I never tire of the taste of mead," Odin said. "Some of the alcoholic drinks you people come up with are truly monstrous, but it seems some of you have a real gift for making honey mead." He looked at me, then back to the bottle. "I must speak to Aegir again," he said. "I have been asking for his recipes and production methods for ages to no avail, but he seems to pass these out to mortals with impunity."

Thor laughed, and we all looked at him. "Maybe the mortals have just discovered the secrets for themselves, Father. They can be quite inventive, when they are passionate about something."

Odin considered this a moment, then glanced back to the empty bottle and sniffed it. "It is possible...but it may give me an angle to barter for myself."

I laughed. Everybody looked at me, but they weren't laughing. "I thought that was hilarious," I said sheepishly. The others continued looking at me as though I had recently escaped a mental asylum. Odin smiled, very slightly, and winked.

Then...he handed me the horn. It was a truly ancient thing, with a silver drinking rim and cap and carved with runes, but despite its age it was well cared for and in pristine condition. I handled it with extreme care, barely daring to believe. This thing was legendary. Could this truly be the horn of Odin? If it was, why had he handed it to me?

"I told you that we cannot take the mantle from you, and that is true," Odin said. "It is a mortal's weapon, created to be held by a mortal. It is, by its very nature, intentionally beyond our reach. In order for us to hold it in trust and pass it on to a new bearer, you must give it up freely, of your own will."

I met his eyes again and felt a bone-deep chill pass through me. "Am I going to die?" I asked.

His eyes remained fixed on mine and he said, "Not from this."

"What will happen to me?" I asked.

I could see him choosing his words carefully. "That is not clear," he said. "You have held on to the mantle far longer than other bearers. It has likely changed parts of you permanently. You may not even notice its absence for some time. After all, your experience is your own, as are your memories. The mantle is merely a purpose-built framework to provide insight. Likely, you will turn the drive to your own pursuits: as a craftsman, a storyteller, a musician, and yes, a warrior for good. You want to be a parent, to help people, and so many other things. Your path is not clear because it is your own. Such is the nature of free will."

"I can accept that," I said. He nodded. "How do I do this?" I asked.

"All power passes from one to another by oath," he said. "Swearing ceremonies are a favorite means of doing this in modern society, but nothing so formal is required here. Simply *will* it done and take a drink from the horn. We will all drink after you in witness."

I closed my eyes and visualized the mantle as two pieces: an armored helm and a sword. In my mind, I held out the helm to Odin. "Do you promise to pass this mantle to a willing and worthy mortal, and not to use it yourself?" I asked.

I heard Odin answer gravely, "I do. I give you my word."

I handed him the helm and unstrapped the sword from my mental side. I offered it out to him and felt him take it. "It is done," I said. I took a weary drink of the mead, then opened my eyes and passed the horn back to Odin. He also took a drink, then held up the horn and said, "It is done." He passed the horn to Thor, who did the same thing and then tilted the horn down for the ravens to drink. The horn went back to Odin, who finished it off with relish.

I sat there, feeling...mostly the same. I did have the sick little feeling in my gut that I had failed somehow. I looked down at the table and tears welled in my eyes. I wasn't sad, really. Just angry at myself, disappointed at my failure. Yes, I had helped some people, saved some people. Maybe even as many as they had told me. But that didn't change the fact that the insidious evil I had seen was still out there, still hurting people. It didn't change the fact that I had been broken, had failed to maintain control of the mantle, and that now they were all still at risk. Odin would keep his word. He would pass the mantle to a worthy bearer.

It didn't change the fact that I had failed my wife and daughter, so long ago and through the ages.

It finally made sense. I felt like I had been slapped with a brick. *That's* what I was seeking salvation for. I still felt guilty for not saving them, for not being there when they needed me. I had never been able to forgive myself for that tragedy, and I didn't believe anyone else could either. I didn't feel worthy of forgiveness, not for that. No wonder I had held onto the mantle for so long. It gave me a purpose to focus on, a way to feel like I was doing some good...to pay for my mistakes.

*My mistakes....*

"Their deaths were not your fault, son," said Odin.

I looked up sharply and saw that they were all looking at me again. They were all straight-faced. I looked directly at Odin and said, "It was."

He shook his head gently. "No, it was not," he said. "None of that was your...."

"It was!" I shouted before I could think it through. Oops. I softened my voice as much as I could and croaked, "If I hadn't been out hunting...."

"...to feed your family?" Thor finished with a question. I glared at him, but he didn't flinch. He continued, "How many other times had you left them at home while you hunted or fished for food, or cut firewood, or traveled to help your neighbors plant and harvest their crops? Do you even know? You left them at home at least twice every month, sometimes more. You were doing that one time what you had done many times before: whatever it took to provide for your family."

"They were attacked while I was gone," I said morosely.

"Of course they were," said Odin. "Cowards always attack when they think there will be no resistance." He met my eyes and said, "They were wrong in this case, but that has escaped your notice." I raised an eyebrow. "You trained your wife well. Her bow felled several of their number before they even knew they were under attack. Why do you think they set your house on fire?"

I had never considered that before. My wife had died fighting.

"You also raised your daughter with a very good example to follow," he continued. "How many times had you used your sword to banish monsters from her room, and laid your shield over her so she could sleep feeling protected?" He paused for just a moment to let that sink in. "She was a strong and somewhat precocious little girl. She wanted more than anything to be just like her Papa, to defend the innocent and helpless. She brought her mother all the arrows she could find, but her mother was very obviously not defenseless. So, she ran to your room and got her mother's sword. It was too heavy for her, so she settled for a dagger instead, and went to defend the only innocents she knew about."

"The chickens," I sobbed. "She loved those chickens."

Odin nodded, and then laughed. At my shocked and hard glare he held up a hand and said, "My apologies. Her defense of those chickens was one of the most glorious battles I have ever witnessed. It took three grown men to take her, and she took one of them with a vicious stab to the wiggly bits, and another with a fine kick to the same region." He belted out another hearty laugh, and everybody joined him – even me, though a bit weakly.

"She also gave those other children hope," he said. "She convinced them to not give up, to always look for escape, to be ready for any opportunity for victory. She knew that you were coming."

Fresh tears rolled down my cheeks. "I didn't get there in time to save her," I said.

"You mistake my words as blame," Odin said. "They are no such thing. At that point, she had no illusions about her fate. She had heard the cowards talking about her, and she knew her time was short. She knew that you were coming, and she also knew you would not be in time to save her. Rather than simply accept this meekly, she chose to pass on her courage to the other children...and after you rescued them, they passed that same courage on to their children." He paused for a moment, then said fiercely, "*That* was her legacy. It has saved uncounted lives."

I held his eyes a moment more, then nodded and looked back down at the table.

"The time for blaming yourself and mourning over them is long past," said Thor. "You will never be able to bring them back. What was is no more. It is meant to be that way."

I was sobbing again, feeling like my world had been irreparably shattered. "Are they happy?" I asked. "I only wanted to make up for the horrors they went through."

Odin looked at the two ravens and they hopped up his outstretched arm to his shoulders. He turned his eyes back to me and asked, "Do you want to see them?"

I wiped my eyes and nodded. Odin stretched out his left hand to me. Without taking my eyes from his, I took his hand.

# Chapter Twenty-Four

T he sensation that took me at that instant is nigh indescribable. It was like having all the breath instantly sucked out of me, forcing me to shut my eyes for just a brief moment. When I opened my eyes again I gasped – not only because I desperately needed a breath, but because we were in a totally different place. We were standing on a narrow street, bordered on one side by houses and on the other side by a large park next to a river. Odin turned to me and said, "There are a few things you should know before we go see your wife."

"Okay," I said, listening closely.

"First, we are not actually here in a physical sense, so the people around us cannot see or hear us," he said. "We cannot interact with them. I believe you know this phenomenon as 'remote viewing.' Do you understand that?"

"Yes," I replied.

"Good," he said. "Second, she does not remember any of the things that you do. She set aside her former lives, and indeed has no interest in remembering...given what you now know, you can hardly blame her."

I nodded again.

Odin returned the nod and said, "Finally – and this may be painful for you – she is no longer your wife. She has no clear memory of you at all, though she has seen you occasionally in dreams, mostly in her younger years. You do not yet realize it, but you provided a good example for her, too." He placed a hand on my shoulder. "Still, the two of you are separated by millennia, and you need to understand and respect that. Do you understand?"

"Yes," I choked out.

Odin nodded and then gestured across the street to the park. We walked to the gate and through it and began to cross a neatly manicured lawn on the banks of the slow, meandering river. "By the way, we are now in Denmark, so I will translate for you," he said. He touched my temple with his right pointer finger and I felt a brief, sharp stab of agony. We continued across the lawn toward a woman sitting on a park bench by the waterside.

When we reached her and walked around the bench to the front, I finally saw her face. I gasped again. She looked a little different, but not overwhelmingly so. She was smiling, watching the sunset behind us. She looked happy, content.

Out of nowhere, a dog bounded around the bench and jumped up at her. She gave a peal of happy laughter, turning her face aside to accept the dog's kisses on her cheek, and ruffled his fur behind his ears. The dog's wagging tail nearly passed through my legs, so I took a small step backward. "Hey, Buddy!" she laughed out. "Did you have a good time at doggy daycare?" The dog, a husky, gave a little yip and wagged his tail even more vigorously. She laughed some more.

That's when a little boy came running up to her and gave her a little kiss and a big hug. "Hi, Mom!" he said. He was about nine or ten years old, with the same sandy blonde hair and sharp features she had. He sat down next to his mother and began excitedly talking to her about what he had learned in school.

A man approached the woman from behind and leaned down to whisper something in her ear. She smiled even wider with a giggle and a little glitter in her eyes and turned her head to give the man a kiss. Odin had been right. This was difficult to watch, but not because I was in any way possessive of her.

All I had ever wanted was to know whether she was okay, and happy. She looked very happy indeed. This just felt a little...voyeuristic. I took one last look at the woman I had once known as my wife, and then looked back to Odin.

"He is a good man, and he takes very good care of his family," he said. "She loves him, and their son, and also the family pet, very much. She is quite content. Are you satisfied?"

I nodded. Odin held out his hand again and I took it. Even prepared for the sensation, it wasn't any less startling or uncomfortable.

When I opened my eyes and gasped in air again, I froze. I was standing inside the small but cozy log home I had watched burn in one of my memories. In a little bed in front of us, my daughter was sleeping, clutching the little wooden chicken with its mismatched assortment of feathers tied on. She looked very peaceful. Despite being asleep, she had a giddy little smile on her face. The sight made me smile, too.

I heard...my wife. Calling from the hearth. Not in an alarming way, just the call of a wife and mother rousting everyone out of bed. The little girl's eyes snapped open and she jumped up out of the bed, put on her sandals, grabbed a small basket, and went pitter-pattering out of the room. I looked at Odin and he shrugged with a small smile. "This was the happiest time of her life. She *loves* this time, and this day in particular. A new batch of baby chicks are to be born today."

We walked out of her room and into the kitchen and dining area. The little girl was helping her mother cook eggs and sausages. I saw myself walk out of the other room, and just about shit my ghostly pants. Odin whispered to me, "The only moment that matters is *now*," as though this would explain everything.

We watched her the whole day: eating breakfast, "helping" with the chickens, dancing around in a fit of excited giggles every time a new chick pecked its way out of a shell, eating lunch, helping feed all the animals, working with her mother in the garden, and getting her Papa to tell her a story at bedtime. I continued watching her long after she had fallen asleep, snuggling up to the little wooden chicken and smiling. She was very happy, and at peace.

I turned and walked out of the house, to find Odin staring up at the stars. I joined him in watching the beautiful display. "Is this...heaven?" I asked.

"It is for her," he replied.

"Thank you," I said.

He nodded and replied, "You are most welcome." He turned to me and said, "It really was not your fault, any of it. You have seen for yourself that neither of them holds any ill will toward you. Nobody blames you for what happened, and no mistakes were made

– not by them, and not by you. It was just life. The Darkness twisted the individuals who committed the acts of evil, and you avenged those acts. You may not realize it yet, but even the individuals who committed those acts were victims, mostly of their own weakness. Your acts of vengeance did three things: addressed the injustices they had committed, removed the threat they represented, and freed their souls from the torment of the Darkness to seek redemption."

I was a bit shocked. "You mean…I did them a favor?"

"I doubt they saw it that way," he replied. "Anyone who considers being stabbed, hacked, and burned a favor clearly has something wrong with them." He chuckled, and I joined him. "I would say instead that you did them a service. It is extraordinarily difficult to see the forest when you are lower than the trees. The only way to see the forest is to rise above the trees. For mortal beings, this means death: getting away from the moment by moment toils of life, getting away from the constant decision-making process that leads one to choose good or evil, and getting to a place where one can clearly see the distinction between the Darkness and the Light."

"May I ask something…uncomfortable?" I asked him.

He peered at me out of the corner of his eyes. "You have been asking this same question your entire life," he said softly.

"Yes," I said. "I am weary of Wandering, of being constantly fearful that I will burn for eternity if I am not a member of the...'correct'...religion. It is a possibility that haunts my every step. I seek the truth about the Divine. One would think that speaking directly with one's deity would sweep away all doubts, but...."

Odin laughed. I stood paralyzed. Surely, this was my end. Why else bring me to see that my wife and daughter were okay? I began to tremble but made myself stand tall. If I was going to meet my death, I could think of no better way and no better place.

Still chuckling, Odin asked, "Deity?" He dabbed at his eyes with a handkerchief and glanced aside at me. "Which am I this century? The god of death, war, or poetry?"

I hadn't expected this. "Uhh...all three of those, and more."

"Really?" he asked. I nodded. He seemed taken aback for a moment, then let another small chuckle escape. "I must confess it is nice to have a justification for my drinking habit beyond 'I just like the taste of mead.' I will have to remember that excuse the next time Frigg gives me the infamous 'wife says no' look at dinner. 'It makes me more powerful' sounds much better. Thank you for that." He smiled a little, and I returned it sheepishly. I really had no idea how to react to this.

"Whenever you think about spirituality, religion, and faith, it always comes back to a single, loaded question," he said. "Do you know the question?"

I considered this and asked the oldest question I could remember. "Why am I here?"

"Indeed," Odin said. "A single question that attempts to address two key things: creation and purpose."

I tilted my head a little to one side, trying to think my way clearly through this. Odin didn't make me wait. "Our own creation story starts how?" he asked. "Do you know the old stories?"

"It began with Niflheim and Muspellheim coming together in Ginnungagap," I said. "A land of ice and a land of fire meeting in the void. The fire began to melt the ice, and a cow – named Audhumla – licked the ice to feed herself, freeing the first being, a giant...named...."

Odin was looking at me with a slightly confused demeanor. "You really do not see any issues with that story?"

"Well..." I said. "It is a *bit* strange, but...."

"So, you can't believe that an all-powerful being gave of himself to create everything," Odin asked, "but you can believe that a cow licked my grandfather out of an ice block like some kind of grotesque snow-cone?"

"Well, when you put it like that...."

"I bet the Hindus *love* that story," he said. "But you are missing the point. It does not make any sense. Where did Niflheim and Muspellheim come from? Where did that cow come from? Where did my grandfather come from, and how did he get into that ice?"

"I...don't know," I admitted.

"I do," he said. "Drunk skalds, wanting more food and drink."

Shocked, I said, "I see your point. That's not a story about creation, because there were already places and beings."

Odin nodded. "The biggest danger of an oral tradition like ours is that people begin to embellish the stories, or just make them up in an attempt to answer intellectual questions they have not considered before." He sighed. "Drunk skalds have done more damage to society than you know."

"So, you're saying that you are *not* a god?" I asked, wondering if it would be my last question.

He turned to face me and put a hand on my shoulder. I met his eyes, trying to hold the fear and confusion inside. "Can gods die?" he asked.

I shook my head slowly. "And yet my death was told in the same tales as Thor's, Baldur's, and all the rest," he said. "'The doom of the gods,' they call it." He gestured to a nearby canoe that lay upside down on logs, and I sat down on it. He joined me.

"Some of the stories, at least some parts of them, are absolutely true," he said. "I did do some very extraordinary things, as did my children and friends and other family. So did you, as you have seen over the past couple of weeks. My mother was a giantess, as were Thor and Loki's mothers."

"Wait," I said. "The giants are real?"

He smiled. "They are…or were," he said. "They were all over Midgard in those days." He paused and put some tobacco in a long-stemmed pipe, then lit it and took a few puffs before offering it to me. I had no idea where he was getting all this stuff but decided to indulge myself. How many opportunities would I have to smoke a pipe with Odin? I took a couple of puffs on the pipe and found the smoke very smooth and relaxing. "You should take my son's advice," he said into the silence of the still night. "Giants are clearly mentioned in the Bible, right in the first book."

"I'm confused," I said, handing the pipe back to him. "You tell me you are not a god, but…," I gestured around us and at his pipe. "There is clearly more to you than mere mortals could achieve!"

"Why would you think that?" he asked. "Because I am performing dazzling feats of what is clearly magic?" He drew on the pipe again and blew the smoke out in a billowing cloud that hung suspended in the chilly night air. "You are capable of all the things I am doing. All human beings are capable of these things, and more. That is almost a direct quote from Yeshua."

My next question just exploded out without checking in with my brain first. "Then why can you do it, and we can't?"

"Have you tried?" was his immediate retort. At my obvious consternation, he chuckled softly. "First, you must understand that humanity is very, very old; far older than you have been told. I am simply a man. My mother and father were human. My brothers are human. I am physically no different than you or any other mortal. I had many questions when I was young, the same as you, and I chased the answers to those questions...and all the new questions those answers gave rise to. I was wholly consumed by the pursuit of knowledge and wisdom. I even took up a mantle that was aligned with my aims – the mantle of the Guide – and it is a mantle I bear to this very day. I have been around a very, very long time. I have picked up a few things over my many lives. As have you."

I couldn't believe what I was hearing, even though it made perfect sense. Except the thing he had said about Yeshua. I asked him about it.

"He said quite plainly that all who believe in Him are capable of the works He did, and more," he said. "I think that is in the book of John." He turned his head to face me and asked, "Do you know who he is?"

"Yeshua?" I asked. He nodded. "I think His original name was Yeshua Ben-Hur, which makes sense given the time and place of His birth: the Romans ruled in those days."

"Correct," he said, "but I was referring to his titles."

I thought about that for a moment. "You mean how he is called the Savior, the Messiah, and the Son of God," I said.

He looked right back at me and said softly, "In scripture, He is most commonly referred to as the 'Son of Man.'"

My jaw dropped. "The Son of...."

"Man," Odin finished for me. "His innate divinity is implied through the story of his conception and birth, but it was actually voted on by the Council of Nicea, leading to the Nicence Creed, which formally declares Him both fully man and fully God. What he says throughout the gospel is some variation of 'I am in the Father, and the Father is in me.'" He narrowed his eyes, the pipe stem hovering close to his lips. "Do you see it?"

"I think so," I said. "He was meant to be a perfect example for us, and therefore had to be a typical mortal. Still, to be a perfect example, not mired in the standard parent/child relationships, He had to be...well, *begotten*, by the Father." I thought a little more and said, "If memory serves, I remember hearing that we are *all* children of God...." Just like that, the pieces fit together. "So, the Creator gave of Himself to create us as immortal souls – 'the Father is in me' – and Yeshua, as a perfect example, lived completely within the Law and trusted completely in his Father...'I am in the Father.'"

Odin looked at me and said quietly, "The mantle that you carried for so long was never meant for you. You carried it well, and you did an immeasurable amount of good, but you are far better suited for a mantle similar to the one I carry. A mantle of knowledge and wisdom." He puffed on the pipe, appraising me. It was distinctly uncomfortable.

"You mean to say that we are all capable of the same things Christ did...and more?" I asked.

"No," he replied. "I mean to say, as Yeshua said, that we are all *born* to do it. You said it yourself not long ago, and you have more reason than most to know, since you have experienced this firsthand: power does not change hands without consequence. If the Creator is power, and gave of Himself to create us, then the power of creation lives within all of us. He gave us a set of rules to live by that would ensure a good society, but without action to build and shape that society they are just another set of rules. Given that people have a penchant for breaking rules...well, you see the problem."

I tried to suss out why this would be hidden. If we really had this kind of birthright, why would it be hidden from us....

I gasped. It couldn't be true...but it was the only explanation that made any sense.

"It's a control mechanism," I breathed. Odin watched me pensively, puffing on his pipe. "Religion is a way to control the population. It's a framework of rules that the individual must follow to go to the good place, and disobedience means you go to the bad place...only the bad place isn't explicitly defined. Come to think of it, the good place isn't explicitly defined, either. Instead, both destinations are up for a certain amount of interpretation."

Odin had begun to smile, just a bit. "You begin to see," he said. "Please continue."

I obliged him. "The only things spelled out definitively are the rules, and those may only be interpreted by the appointed leaders of the religion. Not that the rules need to be interpreted, but there can only be one principal in a school."

I looked up at Odin, and he raised the pipe slightly in a kind of toast. His smile broadened, and he said, "You are quite good with metaphors. I am enjoying them. Keep going. You are almost there."

I thought a moment more. "Yeshua didn't just come to show us a good example. He was the wildcard, an attempt to bring the truth to light. The truth that we are all God's children, and that we have an opportunity to create a good, loving society in the mortal world...Heaven on Earth. The truth that the nature of free will gives us the potential for a darker nature, which we must be diligent to avoid. Some call it the Adversary, some call it the Darkness. Why does power corrupt? Because we have the power to *choose* corruption. It's not an external force, it's part of us. The same as the ability to *choose* goodness and righteousness. Adam and Eve were booted out of Eden not because they ate an apple, but because they took knowledge before they could learn how to use it responsibly."

"Now," Odin said, "you begin to see the scope of the truth." He tapped out the spent ashes from the pipe and stood to face me. "It is a story as old as humanity and holds as true now as it did when it was first told. Human beings were created as the ultimate creation: one that could continue to create. Yet before they could learn to do this responsibly, they chose to take the knowledge of good and evil – the true mystery of free will – and became the masters of their own fates, without really understanding what that could mean. In doing so, they separated themselves from God. They became mortal in the sense that they would have to suffer physical death – a means of forcibly limiting the evil one could do – and were given consequences for choosing to commit evil acts as a means of deterrence."

"I understand," I said.

"Did you know that there is only one sin that will not be forgiven?" he asked. I had not heard this, so I shook my head. "It is one of the Ten Commandments, commonly mistranslated as 'you will not take the Lord's name in vain.' The original Hebrew states 'you will not *carry* the Lord's name in vain.' The only sin that will not be forgiven is choosing to do evil in the name of God, specifically because it tarnishes the name of God and makes it difficult for people to trust Him after enduring the consequences of the evil done in His name."

I just sat there, stunned. I closed my eyes and forced myself to think through the implications of this. What he was saying, and what I had experienced over the past couple of weeks, made a very uncomfortable amount of sense. We had botched our first lessons in immortality and power and had been given rules to live by to guide our own learning. We had also been given the original "carrot and stick": the promise of Heaven and the threat of Hell.

It was a lot to take in. God had given us power and the innate intuition to determine right from wrong as a helping hand. We had taken the knowledge of free will, gotten ousted from class, and done some seriously bad things for the next several thousand years. Yeshua had come to show us the truth about who we were and what we were supposed to be doing. He even demonstrated the power we all had within us through healing and told his apostles to do the same. Not a lot of people know that the apostles also healed people and cast out evil. We – not the

Romans, but *we* – had chosen Him for crucifixion. We had consciously chosen to walk a darkling path. Rather than abandon us to the desolate pit we were creating for ourselves, He had made us a promise that he would return and wipe out evil for good.

Why didn't we listen?

Well, some of us had. Some followed Him, even gave their lives over to serving Him. The only problem was the human institution of the Church. Power itself does not corrupt, but the ability to choose the evil option does. Human weakness – weakness of will – does. The Church was an institution composed entirely of mortals, and it acquired an agenda or two over the years, all of them with a single agenda: to acquire and posses power over other mortals. How many monarchies and empires had gotten and kept their power over nations of people simply because the Church had decreed a ruler divinely appointed? In exchange, of course, for wealth and influence over the ruler.

That's when the final pieces of the vast puzzle snapped into place. *Controlled opposition.* Why would they change a reverence for the wisdom of ancestors into a religion? So that their religion, which forbade the worship of other gods, could sweep in and conquer. Christianity was not the issue. Christianity was meant to empower and guide humankind. The Church, however, was a human institution with all the inherent desires and weaknesses of the humans who comprised it. The Church...the Church was a *power grab*. A monumental power grab. The biggest problem? It was *working*.

It had been working for a couple of *millennia*.

We were in far more trouble than we knew.

My eyes snapped open, and I was confused for a moment. I was back in my apartment, looking across the table at Odin. He was looking back at me, and Thor and the two ravens were likewise looking at me.

"You understand it now," Odin said. "Though I think it is important to be very clear here. The institution known as the Church is composed of a large number of mortals. The vast majority of those people are just trying to do good for their fellow humans. They are not *willing* participants in the sense that they truly believe they are doing something good. They are called to do what they do. Still, they are raised in a system that demands obedience to the rules of that system. They are not the enemy. The system that sets the rules and teaches them what to believe, what to think, what to teach others...the *system*, the *Church*, is the enemy. Not the ones who serve it, but the institution, the establishment. Do you understand?"

I nodded. I got even more nervous, though. One of the reasons for the establishment was the ability to retain full-time ministry staff. Being a minister, pastor, priest, or preacher wasn't exactly a life of luxury – at least, most times it wasn't – but it was stable. It was a steady paycheck. It was a job.

*There it was, plain as day.*

It was never meant to be a job. It was meant to be a service. All of the preachers and teachers of the Bible, except those that were part of the establishment, were poor or destitute, giving freely of their time to teach others. Government was meant to be the same way: a service, people giving their time and effort freely to look out for the common good. The most expedient means of corrupting that kind of power was to turn it into a paid profession...to shift the focus from serving others to serving oneself.

Everybody was still looking at me. I blinked, swallowed, and shook my head.

"You have a lot to think about," said Odin. "We will leave you to it." He stood up, and the two ravens took their places on his shoulders. Thor also stood. They all headed for the door.

"Wait!" I said. "What am I supposed to do with this information?"

"You are seeking salvation for something you did not do, from an institution that cannot give it," Odin said. "You have the answers you sought, and now *you* must decide what to do with those answers. We can guide you no farther."

"Can I ask a couple more questions about you?" I asked.

He stopped and turned around just inside my doorway. Thor waited beside him.

I cleared my throat and decided to just ask. "You learned the secret of the runes...."

Odin belted out a deep, hearty belly laugh. It startled me. The laugh went on for a good minute. Thor was laughing too. The ravens were cackling and hopping foot to foot. I didn't get the joke. "What are the runes?" Odin finally chuckled out.

I stood silent, still not catching on. Odin didn't make me wait long.

"They are letters, an alphabet," he said through another laugh. "The best way to speak truth and wisdom to future generations is to *write it down*." He laughed heartily again and began wheezing a little with the effort of it. He dabbed at his eyes with that same white handkerchief. "You underestimate the simple charm of an oral tradition, my friend. Literacy in such a society is a very rare thing. I learned to read and write, so I could pass down some of what I had learned."

"That's all?" I asked. I couldn't believe it. Surely there was more to it than that.

Odin got very serious for a moment. "Never underestimate the simple and profound power of literacy," he said. "Though I must warn you: reading and writing by candlelight can be terribly hard on the eyes." He tapped the leather eyepatch and burst out into more laughter. I laughed, too. It was funny. "You have one more question for me," he said, reining in his laughter.

I didn't know how to phrase this one, so I just asked it. "How did you know that I would need this kind of guidance?" I noticed that Huginn was shaking his head as he hung it in silence. Muninn was looking a little perplexed.

Odin reached out his hand to me, and I grasped it and shook it. He winked with his good eye and said softly, "A little bird told me."

Muninn sighed and said, "That never gets old." We all laughed. It felt good.

"Thank you all," I said. They all nodded and turned to leave my apartment, except Thor. He stepped forward and shook my hand, then pulled me into a hug. "I have not seen him laugh like that in a long, long time," he said. "Thank you for that, Brother."

I nodded as he stepped back and gave me a fierce smile. "Will I ever see you again?" I asked.

His face looked almost confused. "We are your ancestors," he answered. "We are always with you. If you have need of us, you need only call." He patted my shoulder heftily, then turned and walked out after his father.

# About the Author

I'm a strange bird. I've spent my whole life so far intensely focused on religion and spirituality. Maybe too intensely. Still, I've learned a *lot* about what various peoples around the world believe. I think my intense focus has done me some good...and I hope it does others some good, too.

Including you.

If you have found this book entertaining, or helpful, or valuable in some way, please consider leaving me a review and recommending it to others.

Thank you for reading!